That's Life.

That's Life.

An Autobiography

GORDON HILL

ISBN: 1542744326
ISBN 13: 9781542744324
Library of Congress Control Number: 2017904130
CreateSpace Independent Publishing Platform
North Charleston, South Carolina

<u>Inspired By:</u>
Francis Mallmann
Trymaine Lee
Nick Candito
Casey Neistat
Victor Cruz
Sean Dougherty
Courtland Bragg
Peter Elliott
Robert Greene
Jake Chamseddine

This book isn't about football; it's about the journey football took me on and the people I met along the way.

For You.

True understanding is to see the events of life in this way: "You are here for my benefit, though rumor paints you otherwise." And everything is turned to one's advantage when he greets a situation like this: You are the very thing I was looking for. Truly whatever arises in life is the right material to bring about your growth and the growth of those around you. This, in a word, is art—and this art called "life" is a practice suitable to both men and gods. Everything contains some special purpose and a hidden blessing; what then could be strange or arduous when all of life is here to greet you like an old and faithful friend?

—Marcus Aurelius

Table of Contents

Introduction

This book is unique and special to me. I don't know how to describe it or put it into a genre, because I think it covers a couple of different bases. It's a memoir, an autobiography, and an appreciation all wrapped up into one. To put it in simpler terms, it's really just a conversation with me. I don't want to talk *at* you; I want to talk *to* you. Regardless, I hope you enjoy it, and if you don't, that's OK too. I didn't write it for anyone else but myself, to be honest, but once the book was done, I thought, "Why not share it with people?"

Below is a thought of mine about the book. I feel that it's important to share to help you better understand what you're about to dive into:

If it takes a village to raise a child, well then, this book is the story about the village.

The Zone

You know that feeling of being in control of something? As if no matter what happens, you know that you can't be stopped? Well, I know that feeling very well. I first learned how to control that feeling out on the football field when I was six years old. We were playing the Williamstown Warriors, and the field was muddy. But that didn't matter to me, because I knew no matter what I did on that field that night, it was going to work. Why? I don't know; it just always did. For some people, it always does. I guess you can call this feeling "the zone"; at least that's how many other athletes refer to it.

Anyway, in this game against the Warriors, I played quarterback for the Winslow Maullers. I wore number 24. Now that I'm older, I think it's silly for a quarterback to wear a number like that. Usually, a number in the twenties would go to a running back or a defensive back. But I was young; I didn't know any better. Plus it was my first number in football, and I loved it.

Against the Warriors that night, I scored three touchdowns, and none of them were passing, believe it or not. I know it's a little unconventional for a QB, right? I knew that though, even at the age of six. I don't know why the coaches ever put me at QB my first year in football. Maybe they thought I was smart enough to know all the plays. Or maybe they thought I had some leadership qualities and was a good fit for the position.

Regardless of their reasons, I actually wanted to play running back, because at six I thought I was the fastest kid around. So every once in a while, I would mess up the running plays on purpose so I could run the ball myself. Why'd I do it? I don't know. I think it was because I wanted to win, and I knew if I ran the ball, I could score at will. So that's what I did. I'd notice that after the botched execution of the original play, my coaches weren't really mad at me. They would just kind of laugh and say, "Great play, Gordon," when I got to the sideline after a touchdown. Their reactions made me happy because they showed me that what I was doing was OK.

We ended up blowing the Williamstown Warriors out that year. Actually, we beat every team that year, even a team that was a year older than all of us. But the reason I focused on this particular game against the Warriors is because that was the moment I learned that this game called football came easy to me and that I had control. Not only that, but it was fun. And fun is what is most important for a six-year-old.

I want to mention the person who made me fall in love with football in the first place. Believe it or not, it was Michael Vick. Now that I think about it, he may also be the reason behind me playing QB. I remember this black freshman quarterback from Newport News, Virginia, starting for the Virginia Tech Hokies. Like pretty much everyone else who witnessed Mike Vick play in college, I was amazed. He made the game look so effortless and so fun. He'd drop back and scramble out the pocket, and in a flash he'd be down the sideline for a sixty-yard TD. That was it; that was all I needed to see to be 100 percent sold on the game of football. I loved it! For those who don't know me personally, to this day I'm still a die-hard Virginia Tech Hokie fan, all because of MV7 and what he did in college. So if you ever read this book, Mike, thank you.

YOUNG KINGS

It was now my second year of playing football, and I was on the seventy-pound A team for the Winslow Maullers. I was only seven years old, but my football acumen was off the charts. I'm not trying to sound cocky or anything; I was just aware, at that young age, of my great understanding of the game and of what we had to do to be successful.

However, I wasn't alone in having this great understanding at this young age. I had a teammate named William Belton, but everyone called him Bill. He also understood what we needed to do to be successful as a winning team. At the age of seven, we may not have grasped the idea of different blocking schemes and things like that. However, we did know that as long as we ran as fast as we could while not getting tackled by anyone on the other team, we would win every game. It sounds simple, but that's how we viewed the game at seven. With that idea in our minds, we were unstoppable; we had control.

Throughout the preseason, I watched Bill at practice and thought, "Wow, this kid is really, really good." When I say he was a good player, I mean Bill could do anything and be great at it. As a running back, Bill would score at will by using either his top-end speed, his elaborate juke moves, or his vision—which was second to none. On defense, Bill played defensive end and was literally unstoppable. He just couldn't be blocked. Bill was the best player I had ever seen play the game of football at that point in my life. Now, I know what some of you are thinking: "Wow, Gordon is really talking this Bill guy up." But I just want to give the man his proper introduction into the story. Plus, you have to remember that all these observations and opinions are from seven-year-old me.

That year, Bill and I became great friends, and we dominated on the football field. But we weren't alone. See, we ran a wishbone offense like some of those legendary Oklahoma teams. The key components to our wishbone offense were Rodney Dean at quarterback, Slick at fullback, and Bill and I at the running back positions. With all four of us in the backfield, it was literally "pick your poison" because at any moment, any of us could take it to the house. Rodney was a skinny quarterback, but he was intelligent and had some speed to burn when he needed to use it. Slick was the fullback; he didn't have the typical body type of traditional fullbacks, but he got the job done. What made Slick a great fullback was that he had a lot of heart and would willingly block anybody for Bill and I. I had a lot of respect for Slick because his position wasn't that glamorous and he didn't get the ball that often.

The person who really made our wishbone offense run like a well-oiled machine was Coach Stone. He was the one who put the backfield together and called all our plays. He was the first coach who pushed me as a player to be better than I already was. It sounds cliché, but he saw greatness in all of us, and he knew we had potential. Coach Stone was hard on us because he knew once we mastered all our plays and got the timing in the backfield down, we could be literally unstoppable. Some days we had a great practice, and he wouldn't have to say much to us. Other days, we would run certain plays over and over until we got them down to a science. Out of all of us in the backfield, Coach Stone was the hardest on Slick. But that was because Slick was his son. You know how you hear stories of how the coach's son is the star of the team and gets the ball all the time? Coach Stone wouldn't do that, and I really appreciated him for that. He treated all of us like his own children; that was just the type of bond we all had. Believe it or not, to this very day Coach Stone is one of my favorite coaches I have ever had, and I have never forgotten some of the things he taught me.

I remember one day overhearing some of the parents at practice talk about Coach Stone. Initially I couldn't understand what they were saying, but then I heard them talking about him drinking and possibly being under the influence at our practices. I didn't care what Coach Stone was drinking or even whether he was drunk. When he stepped on the field, he was all business, and he would help us become successful. To be honest, I was disappointed in those parents for making an accusation like that about my coach. You have to remember that all of us in that backfield were very close to him and looked up to him as a role model. Well, at least I did; I don't want to speak for everyone else. I felt those parents were trying to mess up something great we had, and they may have been a little jealous, so they wanted to bring my coach down. Once again, that's a seven-year-old's way of thinking.

After we got through the adversity in the preseason, it was time to get the regular season started, and we got it started with a bang. Our first couple of games, we literally destroyed our opponents to the point where it was embarrassing for them. I don't remember the final scores of those first three games, but it got so bad that Coach Stone had to take the entire starting backfield out of the game early. However, I do remember all of us putting up mind-blowing numbers, and it was ridiculous. Any given game, Bill would have something like 225+ yards on maybe ten carries and three or four touchdowns. I would have 175+ yards and two or three touchdowns. Slick might have had 75+ yards and a touchdown, and finally Rodney would have a score himself after running one of our infamous quarterback-keeper plays that we would always run on the goal line. We were just a group of kids that couldn't be stopped, and we knew it! For the rest of the regular season, we continued to put up monstrous numbers against every team. Our most impressive feat that season may have been that we didn't let up any points at all! Our defense was relentless, and Bill led it via the defensive end position. I don't remember how many sacks and tackles for loss he had, but it was a ridiculous number. However, all those great stats went out the window when we headed to the playoffs, because every team that made it in was dominant.

We were undefeated going into the playoffs, so we were fortunate enough to have a first-round bye. But after those first-round games played themselves out, we would face the Washington Township Minutemen.

Here's a little background on Washington Township: It was a huge town, and they had to split all the kids in the town into two teams, the Minutemen and the Patriots. From what I understand, when you first start playing football in Township, as many people call it, the two teams have a draft. Once you are picked by one of the teams, you are on that team for life, but there are some exceptions. One, if you have a family member on one of the teams already, you are automatically put on that team. Two, you can be traded between teams in the off-season. In addition, Winslow and Washington Township were slowly creating a rivalry in football that was noticeable not only at the little league level but also in high school. So this was a big game for both of us. My point is that Township was a massive town with a lot of talent because they had a big pool to choose from.

All week at practice, the coaches were telling us that they were a very good team. We heard them, but in the back of all our minds, we knew we had what it took to dominate them. The Minutemen had this star running back named Marcus Gregory, who was running all over the rest of the league. I thought he was all hype, because the coaches kept talking him up but I had never seen him play. Regardless of the hype, it was the conference championship game, and I knew our team would come to play.

On a cold Saturday around noon, we headed to Washington Township to play the Minutemen. On the way there, I thought to myself, if we were the first seed in the playoffs, why did we have to go to their field? It didn't matter, because no matter where we were, my team would be ready. Once we arrived, we got off the bus and started to prepare for the game. While we were on a side field practicing our plays, I looked at Bill, and he had the most calm and collected look on his face. It was as if he knew everything was going to be all right and we were going to hit this field and come out victorious, for sure. It calmed me down because, not going to lie, I was a little nervous.

It was game time! We hit the field, and I looked at the kid my coaches had been talking about all week: Marcus Gregory. He was big! Matter of fact, he was really big for a seven-year-old. As we prepared to kick the ball off first, I was thinking, "I have to tackle this kid?" We kicked the ball off, and it was on! We ended up tackling the ball carrier at the ten-yard line, but I still hadn't gotten my first taste of contact yet. Most football players know what I mean by that first contact you get in a game. It wakes you up, like coffee in the morning. It gets you acclimated with what's going on and gets rid of all your nerves. The next play, I got involved in the tackle. I finally got my first piece of contact, and my nerves went right away. Now, I was locked in and good to go!

On second down, the Minutemen ran the ball, and as usual, we stopped them for a minimal gain. Without a hiccup, we were playing like ourselves, relentless. On third down, everyone knew who was getting the ball: Marcus Gregory, of course. The ball was snapped, and like a missile, Marcus Gregory shot straight down the middle of the field on a run play that gashed a hole in our defense. I played corner, so right away I started my pursuit of Marcus, trying my best to stop him from scoring. It was a legit race to the end zone, and I started to close ground on him. Out of nowhere, around the thirty-yard line, Bill flew by me and was closing fast on Marcus.

In what may be the most unorthodox tackle I have ever seen in my life, Bill threw his right arm over Marcus Gregory's shoulder and took him down at the five-yard line. At that moment, I didn't know whether I was frustrated because Marcus Gregory had just run eighty-five yards down the field on us in one play, or amazed that Bill had come from defensive end, flying by me, to save what could have been the first touchdown ever scored on our team. It was a weird mix of emotions, but regardless, we still had a game to play. I mean, shoot, it was only a couple of minutes into the first quarter.

Two plays later, from the five-yard line, Marcus Gregory scored the first-ever touchdown we let up as a team that year. At that moment, I knew Marcus Gregory was the real deal and we had to stop him to win. I was kind of in shock because letting up a touchdown was something that we never let happen. I remember hearing Township's fans getting excited and cheering. It was weird to me; I had never seen another team's fan section cheering when they played us. But now, we were getting the ball, and if there was one thing we could do, it was score.

That first drive on offense was like many we had that season. A hand-off to me, first down, handoff to Slick, first down, and handoff to Bill for a fifty-yard touchdown. In only a couple of plays, we were back in the end zone, celebrating our teammates' accomplishments. When we got back to the sideline after Bill's touchdown, I looked over to him and saw that same calm and collected look he had in pregame. At that point, I knew we were going to win; not only was Bill focused and locked in, but we all were, and you could see it in our eyes. We had a certain swagger about us that year that couldn't be explained or matched. Whatever it was, you definitely noticed if you saw us play.

The rest of the game, we dominated both offensively and on the defensive side of the ball. With a couple of minutes left in the game, our fans were singing, "Na na na na, na na na na, hey hey hey, good-bye!" It was a great feeling, hearing that. We ended up winning 32–6, and as it did in most other games, our backfield dominated. Bill had three touchdowns, Slick had one, and I had two. Now we were off to play the also-undefeated Washington Township Patriots in the championship game. They were good!

Audubon High School was the host of the championship game, and everyone came out to cheer for his or her respective team. Before I got out of the car, my dad told me that this school was where a quarterback named Joe Flacco went. My dad said he was pretty good, or something like that. At the moment, I didn't care what he was saying, because I was so locked in to the task at hand. But, we all know how great he turned out to be. It was a cold Saturday morning. With every breath, I could see the steam leave my mouth. It was so cold that there was still frost sitting on the tip of each blade of grass, but we didn't care. We just wanted to prove that we were the best team in the league. This was our opportunity, and we weren't going to be denied! But it wouldn't be that easy, because of one player in particular: Charlie Huff.

If you grew up in South Jersey around my time, or even if you raised a child around the same age as me who played football, you definitely knew who Charlie Huff was, or at least you had heard of him. Charlie Huff may have been the most successful and dominant little league football player I have ever seen. The interesting thing about Charlie Huff was that he was one of the smallest guys on the field, so at first glance you might have assumed that he couldn't be that good. But those who judged him before seeing him play made a huge mistake. That kid played with so much heart and effort that he would immediately terminate assumptions and make believers out of people. He made plays that others just couldn't make, and he made it look so easy.

Charlie Huff played quarterback for his team but would always run bootlegs to showcase his talent with the ball in his hands. He also was a great punt returner and kick returner. Basically, if the ball was in his hands, he was a huge threat to the opposing team. He was extremely elusive and agile. Because he was short, he was sometimes hard to find behind the line of scrimmage. To be honest, he was the only person in our league who was as dominant as Bill. Just for the record, in my opinion, Bill was still the best player in the league, for sure. All right, let's get into the game now.

As in the previous game, I was nervous but didn't know where those nerves came from. I was confident we were going to win. I knew my team-mates and I were prepared to stop Charlie Huff, but for some reason I just wasn't sure about something. What was I doubting? Or were these good nerves? I don't know, but I couldn't shake them at all. Stepping on the field before the game was amazing; this was the biggest crowd I had ever played in front of in my young career. I don't know exactly how many people were there, but to me it felt like more than ten thousand. When I walked out for the coin toss with my fellow captains, I could hear the crowd roaring in preparation for the opening kickoff. When we got out to the middle of the field for the coin toss, Charlie Huff and I made eye contact, and I instantly saw he had that same look in his eye Bill always had. He was calm, cool, and confident. It almost seemed as if he wasn't about to be playing a football game, especially one of this magnitude. We lost the coin toss, and the Patriots chose to receive first. Back deep was Charlie Huff, and we knew if he got the ball, we had to be disciplined and stay in our lanes while running down on kickoff. Just as in last game, I was looking for that first piece of contact to get rid of the nerves, and I found it while assisting on the tackle of Charlie.

Now it was time for our defense to go to work against arguably the best offense and single player in the league. We were going to find out whether we were the real deal. You have to remember we had let up only six points all season, and that was the previous week against the Minutemen. I'm not trying to rush the story, but to fast-forward to the important part, the Patriots drove down the field on their first possession. They were now on the five-yard line going in; it was third and goal, and we needed a stop to get the momentum headed in our direction. Charlie stepped under center and started his cadence while scanning the defense. Right away I knew the ball was staying in his hands and he would be running some type of QB keeper. Set…go! Charlie Huff faked the ball to the running back and ran directly into my direction. While out at corner, I noticed that some of my teammates were fooled by the play fake, which left me on an island out wide with Charlie Huff, as he had a two-way go. He had enough room to cut it up inside or bounce the play wide across my face.

I honestly didn't think Charlie was resilient enough to do the latter, so I took an angle I was sure would make him cut it up toward my pursuing teammates. Well, let's just say I myself had doubted Charlie Huff's ability. He juked me so bad I couldn't even play it off. "Touchdown Patriots," I heard over the loudspeaker. I felt disappointed in myself for letting my team down and not doing my job. After that touchdown, I knew it wouldn't be easy as long as number 9 (Charlie Huff) was in the game.

Now, it was time for our engine to get going a little, and we had some special things under the hood. The first two plays, the ball went to Bill. That was all he needed to introduce himself to the Patriot defense. We were back up 7–6 after Bill's sensational runs, and our team got a boost of confidence, as we were ready to get back on defense. Once again, Charlie Huff and the Patriots drove right down the field on us, and it seemed we couldn't crack the code on their offense. They ran an extravagant offense for a bunch of seven-year-olds, but they made it look so easy and effortless. It reminded me of our offense, really.

When the Patriots got back down in the red zone, once again they ran a play headed my way. This time it was a fake speed sweep, where Charlie Huff would fake a handoff to the running back sprinting my way and then follow the pulling guards as well as the running back. It was three on one, and I felt helpless. The two linemen tossed me out of the way as Charlie scored once again to put his team in the lead. After we stopped the Patriots from scoring the extra point, the score was now 12–7, Patriots. We had to answer back, and we knew we would.

Coach Stone called the usual plays that would lead to successful scoring drives, and as normal, they worked. We were driving the ball at will as we just crossed midfield. The call came into the huddle, and Rodney said, "Twenty-six counter on two." That meant the ball was coming to me, and on one of my favorite plays at that. Set…go! The ball was snapped, and I received the handoff from Rodney. I hurried to the six hole, where I met very few defenders. I hurried up to the second line of defenders, where I evaded one of the linebackers. I then met one of the corners out on the perimeter of the defense, where I hit him with a spin move. It was weird because I had never done a spin move in an actual game before. I had tried it while playing with friends and such but never in a game. So when I did the move, it was cool how successful it was. After dodging the corner with the spin move, I was off to the races as the rest of the Patriot defenders pursued me, but they never caught up. Touchdown Maullers! Or so I thought. Once I reached the end zone, I noticed a flag was thrown on the play. The referee called holding on the play, which left me a little frustrated, but you know what? That's life. I couldn't get mad over something that I couldn't control.

With the penalty issued, we now needed a big play to get a first down and keep this drive alive. When Rodney came back to the huddle with the play from Coach Stone, he said, "Repeat the last play, twenty-six counter on two." Coach Stone had a great understanding of deception and how it worked. I mean, it was kind of genius, if you think about it. Who would think we would run the same exact play we had just scored with to help move the chains?

Set…go! Once again, Rodney handed the ball off to me, and I hit the six hole, but this time there wasn't a clear path. When I got to the hole, a defender was awaiting my arrival. Without hesitation, I used one of my homemade juke moves. Once I reached the linebackers, I had a head of steam, so I flew by them. Unfortunately, in the secondary, there were three defensive backs waiting for me at the first down marker. So I lowered my shoulders and tried to power through all of them. When I got up from the pile, the referee said it was a first down. The drive was still alive! We had a healthy set of downs, and we used them wisely. After about five more play calls, we found the end zone again. This time it was Slick who scored the touchdown. I was so happy for him, because he didn't get the ball as much as Bill and I did.

After four quarters of battling the best team we faced all year, we ended up winning 36–12. We were champions! I'll never forget that feeling of all our hard work all year paying off. It's a unique feeling that not everyone experiences in his or her lifetime. It's something special that can be felt only among those other guys who sacrificed time, energy, emotion, blood, sweat, and tears to reach that point. So to all my teammates and coaches who were a part of that year's team, I want to say thank you for everything. You guys helped me understand what it feels like to be on a championship team and what type of work ethic you need to be successful.

Also, I want to give Charlie Huff his due respect. Charlie, if you get a chance to read this book, I just want to say you were definitely one of the best players I've ever played against. You are one hell of a competitor, and you always made me elevate my game when I played you, so thank you.

Now back to the story. Oh yeah, if you haven't figured it out by now, I will be talking directly to certain people throughout the book, so pardon me for that.

After the championship game, our team was honored with the championship trophy in what was a magical moment to seven-year-old me. I remember looking at the trophy and thinking, "Wow, that's ours. We earned that." After the team trophy was given out, next came the individual awards. The first award given out was the Offensive Player of the Year Award. I thought that for sure Bill deserved that award. I mean, he was the best offensive player in the league, hands down. "This year's Offensive Player of the Year Award goes to Gordon Hill!" the commissioner of the league said. I was in shock! I didn't believe it. There was no way in the world that I could have won that award. I mean, I had a pretty good season, but it didn't make any sense to me. Bill deserved that award. I accepted it and was happy in the moment, but a feeling of uncertainty hovered over me.

Next was the award for Defensive Player of the Year, and once again I knew exactly who deserved it. It was Bill. I mean, he was the most dominant defensive player in the league as well, so why didn't he deserve it? Once again, the commissioner of the league went through his brief speech on the credentials needed to win this award. He then said, "This year's Defensive Player of the Year Award goes to William Belton!" I was so happy for Bill, especially since he deserved it. Unconsciously, I guess him winning the Defensive Player of the Year Award made me a little more accepting of the Offensive Player of the Year Award. I guess the league couldn't give one person two trophies or something like that, but whatever. We both shined that afternoon.

After the awards ceremony, something that, in my opinion, was even more disturbing happened. Our coaches brought the team to the side, along with all the parents, and got ready to announce the players who would represent our team in that year's all-star game. I was excited to find out whether I made it that year; I wanted an opportunity to play in another football game. For sure, I knew Bill had already been selected for the all-stars, so we just had to find out who else would represent our team. Our coaches announced the results; they said Hunter Krajewski and Gordon Hill would be representing our team in that year's all-star game.

All right, guys. You already know what I'm about to say. How in the world did Bill not make the all-star team when he was the best player in the league? I mean, the man just won Defensive Player of the Year but isn't on the all-star team? Bill, I'm not trying to gas you right here, but that's like

Michael Jordan winning the MVP Award and then not being in the all-star game. It doesn't make sense, and it didn't make sense to me even at seven years old. I was so skeptical of how that happened. I felt I didn't deserve to go if Bill wasn't going to play in the game. I felt he was cheated.

Now I want to be honest with you. To this day, I remember hearing some parents talking about Bill's character or how he was cocky and how in that sense, I may have been a better representative of our team than he was. But how dare some parents judge a little kid and take an opportunity like that away from him, especially when he deserves it? Plus, they didn't even know him. So how could they say he was cocky or whatever the reasoning was? It was disrespectful, in my opinion, because the adults dictated an outcome and took the kids' work ethic and ability out of it.

Also, I want you guys and girls to know that my father was an assistant coach on this team. Now I don't think the fact that my dad was on the coaching staff made a difference, because my dad was never the type of father who got caught up in the politics of little league sports. However, I still question and think about that moment in my life. What was the real reasoning behind it all? How did they, whoever they are, come up with this decision? It bothered me for a while because it was an injustice to Bill.

I never talked to Bill about the whole incident, and I still haven't. It's in the past now; we were only seven, and I don't think Bill really cares about it. I mean, shoot, he's written his own story, and no one can ever take all those memories from him. Bill, I do want to take some of the blame and say sorry for how that whole situation went down. I know it technically wasn't my fault, but I feel someone needs to say it because, as I said, it just wasn't right. Also, keep writing your story, because there are people watching you, whether it's the little kids who play little league football from Sicklerville to State College, or the kids in high school who saw you have game-winning touchdowns on some of the biggest stages, or just me who watched you as a seven-year-old. I was always looking to see how I could integrate some of your moves into my own game. Trust me: we all did it. We were all watching. You were one of the first people to show me what it means to be elite at this game, and for that, Bill, thank you.

If you were wondering, Bill and I still communicate. We've never had bad blood or anything like that. We have always been in similar circles because of the sport we play. However, our friendship has never been as strong as it was when I was on that seventy-pound Winslow Maullers team. Nowadays, though, we always find time to catch up.

After all the accolades were handed out, everyone got ready for the party my coach hosted at his house. When I first arrived, everyone was down and upset, and I didn't know why. I later found out that while leaving the high school where the game was played, one of my teammates was hit by a car in the parking lot. We were all waiting at the party for some word of his condition. After about twenty-five minutes, he walked through the door with only a couple of bumps and bruises, and finally everyone loosened up and relaxed. That sums up our season and tells you just how unstoppable we were. Not even one of my teammates being hit by a car could stop us.

Mother's Intuition

I want to bring you back a couple of years and give you some backstory before we proceed. Let's go all the way back to seven-month-old me. To understand the importance of the first two chapters and the rest of the book, you have to read this chapter. The people who know me well may understand where I'm going with this. And even if you know a little bit of the story, trust me: you never got all the details. For everyone else, this is a mother's intuition.

It was a normal day, just like any other day of the week. My mom got me ready to head over to the babysitter's; then she got dressed to head to Winslow Township School No. 4, where she taught second grade. Dad worked early mornings and was already out the door, handling multiple jobs at the time.

Mom and I got in the car and drove to Aunt Mel's house. Her real name is Melanie Ann, but everyone calls her Mel. My mom had just gone back to work from maternity leave, so this was only my fourth day at Aunt Mel's house. You can assume it was a Thursday. My aunt was the neighborhood babysitter in the way she watched other kids, not just me.

When we finally arrived at her house and she opened the door, my mom noticed something different from the previous three days. While the door was open, she noticed a man on the couch who looked unfamiliar. With hesitation, my mom handed me over to Aunt Mel. She asked my aunt who the man was and whether he would be staying there. Aunt Mel explained that the man was her baby daddy and his girlfriend had kicked him out of his house. See, my aunt is that type of person; she always opens her door for others. Mom left and headed to work, but all day in the back of her mind was an image of me. She had so many thoughts wandering around in her head. What you have to understand is that my parents never planned to put me in a day care; because they wanted me to be around someone they could trust. So by default, my aunt's house was their only option.

After work, my mom came to pick me up. When she rang the doorbell and my aunt had me in her arms, my mom knew something was wrong. The babysitter said I was good and slept most of the day, as I usually did. However, when we got in the car, Mom finally figured out what was wrong with me. I wasn't sucking my fingers, which I did until I was seven (true story). The other thing was that I was very lethargic and showed no emotion and was just lying still in my car seat. We went home, and my mom immediately brought me over to my dad to get his opinion, to see whether he felt anything was wrong with me. My dad said my mom was being overly cautious and he didn't think anything was wrong. My mom didn't agree; she wanted to make sure everything was OK.

After the conversation with my dad, my mom called the family doctor, Dr. Susi David. She is an old Indian lady with a strong accent, which made her hard to understand, even when I got older. Regardless of the accent, that woman is one of the nicest people I've ever met and has one of the biggest hearts. During her conversation with my mother, Dr. David advised my mother to bring me to the emergency room. She told my mom that if she had an instinct that something was wrong with me, she should follow that instinct. So that's what she did. Mom, Dad, and seven-month-old me hopped in the car and went to the emergency room. For about three hours, my parents sat there waiting to hear back from any doctors about my condition. Eventually, a doctor came out and told my parents that after running various tests on me, he thought I was fine and I probably had an ear infection or some type of fever coming on. Three hours to find that out? Really?

Mom wasn't having it though. She wasn't convinced that everything was all right. I still wasn't sucking my fingers, and until I started doing that, my mom was uncertain I was OK. Dad wanted me to go home and rest in my crib so they could see how I acted in the morning. But Mom wanted answers, and she wanted them urgently. All she knew was that her baby wasn't acting like himself and needed to get back to normal. My dad kept stressing his idea to bring me home and let me rest in the comfort of my own house.

Finally, Mom snapped and said, "Nigger, if you don't listen to me! We will not leave this hospital until we find out what's wrong with my son!" After my mom made those comments, my father was all ears and agreed with anything my mom said. If you have ever met my mom, you know she is literally the nicest woman in the world. She never uses curse words and doesn't even like hearing them in music. So when she said what she said, it was obvious she was dead serious. Before my parents decided to leave the hospital, my mom called Aunt Sobrina for her opinion on what the next move should be. My mom valued Aunt Sobrina's opinion because, one, she was a nurse, and two, she was her sister. The two of them demanded to have the hospital keep me overnight so they could run further tests on me.

In order to be released from the hospital, the doctors needed Dr. Davids' authorization. However, she requested I have the an MRI and a CAT scan. After the tests were done, my mom asked for the results but got no response. Minutes later, she noticed that some of the doctors looking after me began to scramble through the hallways. There was a sense of urgency or pep in their step. That made my mom wonder whether something was going on and whether this newfound urgency had to do with me. The doctors weren't telling my parents anything. They would just hurry past them at a brisk tempo. My mom was getting impatient because she could see the concern on these doctors' faces, yet no one was saying anything.

Finally, a doctor came over to my parents with the news. What they found was hemorrhaging and a hematoma on my brain. Basically, I had bleeding of the brain and was losing oxygen to the brain because my brain was drowning in its own blood.

Without letting my mother get a word in, the doctor told my parents that they would have to do emergency surgery at Cooper Hospital in

Camden. Time was of the essence, and my life was literally on the line. I guess you could say it was as if we were in the 1993 NBA finals with three minutes left in the fourth and we were down by twelve points.

The odds weren't in my favor. Originally, they were going to fly me in a helicopter to Cooper Hospital. But that night there was a bad thunderstorm, and they figured it would be too dangerous. The doctors decided to put me in an ambulance and rush me to the hospital that way. My mom and dad were mad because they weren't allowed in the ambulance with me. The doctors told my parents to get to the hospital any way they could and as fast as they could.

That entire trip to Cooper, my mom was thinking, "How did this happen? Where and when did this start? Is my son going to survive this?" You know, the usual stuff you think when your son is battling for his life. Right when I got to Cooper Hospital, they started surgery. My parents were on their way but were still on the road owing to the inclement weather. When they finally got to the hospital, the doctors told them that the injury had come from some form of blunt trauma. That didn't make any sense to my mom, because for the past seven months, I had been under her supervision, and she knew nothing had happened.

Finally my mom thought about the babysitter. That was the only logical explanation for how this could have occurred. Those four days were the only times I had left her sight. Could that have been it? Aunt Mel looked after so many kids, and she was great with them, but what about the man who had been at the house the day before? Could he have had anything to do with it? All these thoughts crossed my mom's mind at that moment. But what was done was done. Questioning anything then was irrelevant. All my parents could do was wait for me to get out of surgery and see what the surgeon said. They weren't in control anymore.

After hours of surgery, my parents finally got word that the procedure was complete. While they were walking to the recovery room, one of the doctors gave my parents the rundown of the procedure they had just completed. They also told my parents that I would most likely be neurologically and mentally impaired for the rest of my life because of the loss of oxygen to my brain. My parents were in shock and didn't know what to say. All they knew was that there was still a chance that I would be a 100 percent healthy person for the rest of my life, and that's all they needed.

For the next seven days, my mom and dad stayed by my side in the ICU while I recovered from brain surgery. I had all types of tubes and wires connected to me to track all types of vitals. Throughout that seven-day period in the hospital, many things happened. First, there was the whole situation with DYFS, the Division of Youth and Family Services. One of the things they do is try to find evidence in any scenarios where there may have been abuse of a minor. They investigated my case, since I was seven months old and had a head-trauma injury. The people who had the finger pointed at them first were my parents. That was standard operating procedure for cases like this, just to ensure the safety of the child. My father wasn't too happy about this, however. They told him that for the time being, my grandparents would have legal custody of me. My dad didn't care what they told him. He said, "I don't care whom you give custody of my son to. He's still coming home with me."

The next problem my parents ran into while at the hospital was racism. Well, at least that's what my mom felt it was. She said being in that hospital was the first time she felt someone was discriminating against her or her family. It first started when doctors and nurses asked her whether my dad was my biological father. Next, they asked her whether my dad had a job. Now, I don't work in the medical field, but I really don't see how that question is applicable in this situation. My mom told my dad what the medical staff was asking her, and he was furious. My dad said that moment was one of the times he felt the most disrespected in his life. So to change the opinions of the people at the hospital, my dad went home and put on his military uniform. See, my dad had been a major in the US Army for a couple of years now. Not only did he have a job, not only was he in the military, but he was a leader of men. To gain the respect of others at the hospital, he felt this was the only option he had. After he wore his uniform to the hospital that day, my parents didn't have another problem for the duration of my stay.

My mom told me that throughout my seven days in the hospital, numerous family and friends came to visit me. Although I'm not old enough to remember anybody who came to the hospital that week, I want to say thank you for the support and prayers. I appreciate it, and my parents do as well.

After those seven days in the ICU, I finally started to show signs that I was myself again. I started to suck my fingers again, and that's when my mom knew things were getting better. After the seventh day, I was discharged from the hospital and could finally go home. My parents were thrilled and relieved I had started to improve. Once I got home, Dr. David called my mom and said I would have to be seen by a neurologist every six months for a couple of years. At my first six-month checkup with the neurologist, the doctors were literally blown away by how well I was doing. They said that based on how much blood and oxygen I had lost, I was for sure going to have some lifelong effects. Well, I guess that wasn't in my plans.

After a while, people who knew I had surgery and saw me a couple of months later started calling me the miracle baby because they couldn't believe I was functioning so well. You know that saying, "Every mom thinks her child is special"? Well, my mom was right. I was special.

I want to clear some things up for the reader. First, I want to talk about Aunt Mel and our relationship. I have no bad blood toward her whatsoever. I was a little kid and don't remember anything from that age. Now, as far as my mom's feelings toward her, they were a little different initially. My mom was angry about what could have happened. However, once I got the surgery and started to recover, my mom forgave Aunt Mel. She realized that there was no point in holding a grudge or being mad about something that couldn't be proven.

One thing my mom did find out years later was that on the day that man was in the house, Aunt Mel left the house for thirty minutes to go food shopping. I'm not saying anything happened within those thirty minutes, but you never know. Years later, as I got a little older, I would even go over to Aunt Mel's house to play with my cousin Stephan. I didn't know my mom was cautious about letting me go over there, but recently she told me that she was at first.

When it comes to the topic of my playing football at six years old, it was a big decision for my mom. She didn't want me to play, for obvious reasons. But one thing I will always respect my mother for is allowing me to play the game I fell in love with, even if she was cringing on every play. See, that's love to me. She knew how upset I would have been if she had said no. I don't know how my life would have been without the game of football. I mean, you guys and girls wouldn't even be reading this book right now if she had said no to football eighteen years ago. I'm so thankful she said yes, and for that, Mom, for letting me go and having some faith, I thank you, and I love you. Oh yeah, and thanks again, Mom, for literally saving my life. A mother's intuition is always right.

THE MIDDLE AGES

Now that I've told you about my brain surgery, you should have a better understanding of that part of my life. Also, I think it's clear how special and how much of a blessing it was for me to be able to play football, and to play at such a high level. We are now at the point I like to call the Middle Ages, when I was at the youthful ages of nine and ten.

I want to start this chapter off in Mr. Kaiser's fifth-grade class. Mr. Kaiser was an interesting fellow who was tall and always wore these shoes called clogs. They were wooden slip-on shoes that made noise with every step he took. However, that's not the reason I'm starting this chapter here. The real reason is something Mr. Kaiser always hung up in his classroom: his Hall of Fame. The Hall of Fame presented all his former students who were grown up and doing well. The person in the Hall of Fame who always stood out in my mind was Ron Dayne. That's right; the 1999 Heisman Trophy winner and I had the same fifth-grade teacher. Call it fate or whatever you want; all I know is I used him as motivation. I sat in the seat right in front of Ron Dayne's picture every single day that year, and every time I saw it, I told myself, "I'm going to make it onto that Hall of Fame one day."

Ron, I never met you, but I want to say thank you for motivating me to get my picture on the wall in Mr. Kaiser's class. Thank you for showing a kid from the same town as you that as long as you work hard enough and stay focused, anything is possible. To keep it real with you, I think I focused in that class more than I did other years because I had that constant reminder of my goal when I looked at your picture.

All right, back to the story. When I was ages nine and ten, football didn't go as well as I wanted it to. During those years, I was bumped up into the hundred-pound division, and I was the youngest on the team. We weren't that good those years. It wasn't because of our talent; we just didn't have the chemistry a successful team needs to win. Not only that, but I also lost a step with the additional weight I gained. I'm not saying I was out of shape, but I still had some baby fat on me, and I wasn't used to carrying the additional weight yet. With all that factored in, my first year on the hundred-pound team, I played only linebacker. I still played running back, but I was the backup on the A team. I'd go in only if someone needed a breather or was injured.

The running backs that year were talented. We had Rasheed Williams and Bill Belton at running back, while Mike Crowley played fullback. Now, you already know about Bill and what he was capable of, but let me tell you about Rasheed Williams. Rasheed, or Sheed, as many of us called him, was the smoothest running back around. He had the most deceiving speed I've ever seen in my life. He ran so smooth that I used to think he was slow because he never looked as if he was running fast. But trust me: the man could flat out play ball, and much like Bill, when he got the ball in his hands, you wanted to watch and see what he would do next.

As I said earlier, that year didn't go too well for our team, and I'm sad to say it, but I didn't care. It wasn't in a malicious way; I'm not saying I'm happy we lost. But at that time in my life, football wasn't my passion. The people who know me really well know the first sport I loved and excelled in was actually wrestling.

Yup, good ol' wrestling. My father first introduced me to the sport of wrestling when I was six years old. He had a passion for the sport and still does to this day. My dad wrestled in high school and college, and he even coached at the collegiate level. It was the sport he really loved, and he taught me just about everything he knew about it. Now when my dad reads this book, trust me: he's going to be smiling from cheek to cheek after reading that last sentence. So Dad, you can stop smiling now. But seriously, he did teach me just about everything when it came to the sport.

When I first started wrestling, I wasn't good at it at all. My first match ever, I was pinned in seconds by a teammate from the Maullers named CJ Sawyer. It was a rude awakening for me, and an introduction of sorts into the competitive world of wrestling. After taking numerous losses my first year, I looked at all those matches as practice and took my gained experience into the next couple of years. I worked my butt off to become successful at the sport, and with my dad pushing me, it was like a perfect storm. See, my dad was living through me since his wrestling career was over. For many years, he'd ask me whether I wanted to compete each weekend at different tournaments throughout the area. I'd say yes because after a while, I got addicted to the success I was having. Now my dad wasn't one of those fathers who force their children to do things that they themselves want to do. Well, he did do that one time, but we'll get to that later in the book. As I said, it was a perfect storm; I liked winning, and he enjoyed helping me become successful.

Over the years, at every single tournament I went to, I would have to face this kid named Adam Schroeder from Washington Township. Yes, that is the same Washington Township I played in football. I told you they had a huge pool of talent since the town was so big. Anyway, every weekend I would make it to the finals in the local tournaments, and for some reason my opponent would always be Adam Schroeder. He was a skinny white kid with bleached-blond hair who could wrestle his butt off. He was a tough competitor, and every week he would bring his A game to the mat. Over a three-year period, Adam and I wrestled each other at least twelve times. I went undefeated against Adam over that span of time, but don't get it twisted. Those were the toughest matches of my life, and regardless of the record between us, he was my rival. I actually was more concerned about facing Adam in the finals of a tournament than I was about facing someone else. That was because he knew my tendencies so well and what to look for. Somehow, I just kept finding different ways to win.

After three years of seeing each other every weekend at wrestling tournaments, Adam and I formed a friendship. It was weird at first for me because he was my rival. I'm sure he would say the same. But at the same time, it was awesome because after a while, we would cheer for each other once we were in different weight classes (hence the mention of me still having some baby fat). Adam, I want to say thanks for being such a great competitor. You taught me how to eliminate complacency because you were always working to beat me. When I trained for my next match, I would have you in the back of my mind, knowing that you were working your hardest to beat me at the next opportunity. Also, you taught me that even though we were competitors on the mat, we could still be friends off it, and for that, thanks again.

With all the tough matches I had locally against Adam, I felt I was ready to take my show on the road. So that's what I did. I asked my dad to enter me into the MAWAs, the huge regional tournament for the Mid-Atlantic Wrestling Association. Ultimately it would determine the best wrestlers in this region of the country. In 2003, when I was nine, I entered the MAWAs undefeated with over seventy-five matches under my belt. I'm not going to lie; I was extremely confident! The first tournament I had to win was a local qualifier for the MAWAs. Believe it or not, I actually had my first loss of the season at this qualifier, to a kid named Brian Lussier from Cherry

Hill, New Jersey. It was ironic I lost in the qualifier. I mean, the kid was good, but I also didn't wrestle my best. I think I needed to get that loss out of my system just to be a little more humble heading into bigger matches in the future. Besides, the top three finishers of the tournament made it to the next level of the MAWAs, so I was locked in with a second-place finish. It hurt a little to lose, but it wasn't the end of the world.

The next round of the MAWAs was held in Salisbury, Maryland, at this huge arena. It was the biggest venue I'd ever competed in, and it made me super excited. One of my best friends, Hakeem Valles, came with me and helped me stay level headed throughout the tournament. When we first entered the arena, the first thing Hakeem and I noticed was the huge arcade area. And trust me: in between my matches, we ran the arcade area! I mean, we were nine, so it was only right. Seriously though, we really went in on those arcade games.

In my first couple of matches, I dominated my opponents. It was easy, but it didn't last long at all. In the later rounds of the tournament, these guys got far better. When I got to the semifinals, I was up against a kid from Maryland named Justin Kozera, the number-one seed from the southern region qualifier. I knew he was talented and I would have to have my mind right entering this match. When the match started, I noticed right away how aggressive he was offensively; I loved that because I was a defensive wrestler. I used to love countering people and using all their effort and energy against them. The match ended up being close, or at least closer than I expected. I won 6–3, but it showed me the quality of wrestlers that I would soon face in the future.

In the finals, I was matched up against Brian Lussier again, the same kid I took my first loss against the previous week. I wasn't nervous entering the match, because I knew the mistakes I had made in our last match and I wouldn't make them again. However, something was different about him. It wasn't his appearance or anything like that. It was something internal. When the match started, I instantly noticed what was different about my opponent this time around. It was his confidence and the way he carried himself. He seemed very sure of himself this time. He had a different bounce in his step, and it came off as cocky to me, so I had to bring him back down to earth a little. See, I knew that last win he had against me was a fluke. I'm not saying that he hadn't won that last match fair and square, but I knew I wasn't at my best. So I took this match personally; I had started to feel disrespected by Brian Lussier. Now, he was a very good wrestler, and I don't want to take that away from him, but I'm just saying his best wasn't better than my best. But talk is cheap, so let's get to the match.

In the first period of the finals, it was a completely defensive battle. Neither one of us wanted to take a chance against the other. We looked like two guys trying to hug each other, because neither one of us wanted to shoot on his opponent. Entering the second period, it was tied 0–0, and I won the coin flip and chose bottom to start the period. I was good at getting away from my opponents, so I always chose to start at the bottom. Like clockwork, I got away from Brian Lussier's attempts to keep me down and took the lead, 1–0, with an escape. Now we were back to square one. Back to the neutral position, and I knew I had to stretch this lead to ensure a victory over this kid. I knew he wasn't quicker than I was, which pretty much told me he wouldn't shoot in on me, so I would have to be the aggressor. I knew I had to use my quicks to solidify this win, so that's what I did. After a couple of hesitation moves and fake shots, I had my opponent a little off his game. When the moment was right, I took my shot and executed what was probably the most flawless double-leg takedown of my career. It was so pretty; Jordan Burroughs would have been impressed. (Some of you may understand the JB reference, others may not, but don't worry; you'll learn about him later in the book.)

After the takedown, I was up 3–0 and starting to take command of the match—or so I thought. My opponent gained his first point by escaping from my grasp, and now the score was 3–1. In the third period, after winning the coin flip for the first time, my opponent had the option to choose top or bottom. After realizing how easy it was to escape from the bottom against me, Brian Lussier chose bottom. I told myself that all I needed to do was hold him down for the entire period, but it wasn't that easy. In a matter of seconds, Brian Lussier once again broke away from me and scored another point, making the match 3–2. I still felt in control, but physical fatigue was setting in a little, and mental fatigue was as strong as could be. I didn't want to be called for stalling, so like the rebel I was back then as a wrestler, I continued to be aggressive, even with the lead. But remember that I knew I was quicker than this guy, so why not, right? We locked arms a couple of times until finally I saw my next opportunity to take a shot. This time it wasn't as clean as the last shot I had taken, but it was just as effective. I had to work a little up my opposition's leg to get my two points, but eventually I got it. With the lead now 5–2 in my favor, my dad told me to continue to be as aggressive as possible to keep my opponent in a defending mind-set. His advice worked, and I came out victorious. I was now one step closer to becoming the best wrestler at my age and weight class in one part of the country.

The final step to make my goal complete brought me to Happy Valley, Pennsylvania. That's right, I was in Penn State country, and it was awesome. When we got to Happy Valley, I was super excited because one of my favorite football players had attended the university. Even though I was back then, and still am, a die-hard Virginia Tech fan, one of my favorite football players ever is Larry Johnson. He was a star running back at Penn State, and while I was in little league football, he was one of the people I would try to imitate on the field. While at Penn State I was like a kid in a candy store. I mean, if you were a football fan at my age, why wouldn't you be? You'd have been on the same campus as arguably the greatest coach in college-football history. RIP to the late great Joe Paterno, and thank you for all you contributed to the game I love.

My family and I stayed at the Nittany Lion Inn, which was a beautiful hotel that sat right on the campus of PSU. Believe it or not, I actually ran into Joe Paterno in the lobby the first night we were staying there. I told him that one day I might be running the ball for the Nittany Lions, and he just smiled and said, "Soon, son. Soon." That was it; that's all he said as he went on his way. Now that I'm older, I really appreciate that brief interaction we had. Not everyone gets an opportunity to talk to one of the greatest football coaches of all time.

The next day it was time to hit the mat and handle the business I had come there for, and that was to win. The first couple of rounds, I easily beat all my opponents. But now I was facing the number-one seed from the western qualifier, and from what I had heard, he was the number-one seed in the United States in my division. So I had to give it my all to win this match. The kid's name was Tom Collins, and he was tall and lanky. We were matched up in the semifinals, so all I had to do was win this to make it to the finals. As the match began, I realized how defensive my opponent was. He wouldn't shoot in on me at all. He was tough to figure out and get a feel for because he was very unorthodox. He had a weird swagger to him, but obviously it worked. I took a couple of shots in on Tom Collins, but right away I was denied. While still at neutral, we finished the first period tied 0–0. He won the coin flip to start the second period and decided to stay neutral. Once again, the entire period he was super defensive and never took a shot on me. I was waiting for a stalling call by the ref, or at least a warning, but I got nothing. Heading into the third period, my dad told me to stay neutral, as it was my turn to decide our starting position. So that's what we did. I remember thinking, "The ref has to hit this guy with a stalling call eventually." I mean, he wasn't doing anything. As the period started, it was a lot more of the same by Tom Collins: stalling. I thought, "How is this kid the number-one ranked wrestler in America when all he does is stand there?" Well, just as in the previous two periods, we ended up finishing the third in a scoreless tie.

Now we were in overtime, and it was sudden death, so the first person to score would win. It was Tom Collins's decision to pick on the coin flip, which he won, and he chose bottom. Right away I got frustrated because I always had trouble keeping my opponents down. In sudden death overtime, the clock was set to thirty seconds. So literally all I had to do to win was keep Tom Collins from escaping for that amount of time. Sounds easy, right? Well, it's not, especially when you're facing the number-one-ranked wrestler in the country. We got in position, and as the whistle was blown, my opponent instantly shot out of his position in an attempt to stand up and escape. As he got to his feet, I grabbed his waist and threw him into the

When Courtland moved, I was excited about the fact that not only would we be able to hang out more but we would also be able to play football together. Over the years, Court, as many of our family members call him, was known as a beast on the defensive side of the ball when it came to football. He had a unique ability to hone in on ball carriers and crush defenders with bone-crushing hits or finesse tackles. Court was a sure tackle, no matter the ball carrier.

Court also played running back or fullback on offense and was a threat with the ball in his hands. If we needed some short yardage, he was our go-to guy. I can honestly say he brought some toughness to our team that year. On defense, Court played anywhere he was needed because he was just that versatile. One game he'd play cornerback, the next linebacker, and sometimes he would just play rover and go where he was needed depending on the game plan that week. The only person I can compare Court to is Troy Polamalu in his prime. He was that x factor on the field that made everyone else's job easier. That's how my cousin Court played. I knew we had the ingredients in place to do something special on the field that year.

After we won our first game of the season, I was hanging out with one of my good friends, Cole Folks, at Donio Park (Donio Park was the venue of our home games; you'll learn more about it later) to catch some of the older kids' games. Since I had just finished playing my game, I was hungry and asked my mom whether Cole and I could walk to Checkers to get some fully loaded fries. Now that I was eleven years old, my mom trusted me a little more and felt I was responsible enough to venture out on my own. Plus, I was with a friend, and Checkers was right down the street. With my football pants still on, I made my way to Checkers with Cole. We were in our own world as we walked up the hill of Donio Park. I forget what we were talking about; all I remember is that we just kept laughing. Then, of course, I started thinking about food and talking about how badly I was going to demolish those fully loaded fries. I mean, they are some good fries, so if you've never tried them, I highly suggest trying them, even though I don't eat french fries nowadays.

While we were on the sidewalk right next to what was then Super-G, a car pulled out of the Super-G parking lot and began to drive right past Cole and I. Kind of awkwardly, a girl in the back seat positioned closest to me made eye contact with me. She was a Hispanic woman, and I noticed all her tattoos. Now that I think of it, everyone in the car was Hispanic. The next thing I knew, that same woman put an AK-47 out of her window and pointed it directly at Cole and I. I stopped walking and pushed Cole behind me to shield his body with mine. I had a weird feeling that I'd never felt before. It was as if I was accepting my death at that moment. I was at peace and wasn't scared. I just thought that if this was my time, then I would let it be. I didn't try running, because they were within ten feet of us and it wouldn't have made a difference. I mean, they had an AK-47. That's an automatic assault rifle that for sure would have caught up with me if I had run. I was fast but not that fast. While I was shielding Cole, the car continued to drive by us. They didn't shoot us, obviously, but before the girl with the gun pulled the weapon back into the car, she let out one of the most evil laughs I've ever heard. It's hard to describe, but it reminded me of the laugh that the Joker from the Batman movies had. I'm not trying to sound overly dramatic, but I sometimes hear that laugh in my head. I don't know why I still hear it or what it means. All I know is that I'm sure whose laugh it is.

Once they were out of range of Cole and I, we just looked at each other in shock. Now I know I said I wasn't scared when the gun was pointed at me, but after the fact, I was shaking uncontrollably for a couple of minutes. Not only that, but I was shaken up from what had just happened, and it made me paranoid. So I kept looking at the oncoming traffic to make sure those people weren't coming back.

Eventually, we made it to Checkers, and we got those fully loaded fries, and yes, they were amazing. They weren't worth risking my life, but I didn't know someone was going to pull a gun on us. All we wanted was some food; we didn't want any problems with anybody. Now that I think back to that moment, I see it was a bad idea to continue walking to Checkers for some fries. We should have just gone back down the hill into Donio Park and gotten food at the concession stand. But we were young; we didn't know any better. Believe it or not, when we went back to the fields to watch the rest of the games, I didn't tell my parents what happened. I don't know why I didn't tell them. I guess when I was eleven years old, it wasn't that important to me. Plus, my mom had just shown me some trust, and I wasn't trying to screw that up with this new information.

I know that part of the story was kind of random, but it was real and a unique moment in my life, so I wanted to share it with you.

After the first win of the season and the Checkers incident were behind me, the team and I got into a groove. We were winning game after game, and you could tell we started to jell as a team. We weren't like that seventy-pound team that won the championship, but we did have a similar bond. The backfield that year was also a great group of guys. We had Josh Wilson at quarterback and Courtland at fullback, and my bro Davon Jones, a.k.a. Nyce, and I were at the running back positions. Josh was a short quarterback with a great understanding of the offense. Court you already know about, and Davon Jones was one of the fastest kids around. We had a good nucleus of talent that year. Game after game, we would find ways to win, whether it was by scoring a lot or playing great defense. That year our team reminded me of the San Antonio Spurs. We had great balance, and you couldn't key on one person, because we all had abilities that contributed to the team's success.

Late in the year, we found ourselves matched up against the Gloucester Township Stallions. They had a lot of offensive firepower, mainly because of one player: Damiere Byrd! I remember hearing about this kid while I was growing up because people would always talk about how fast he was. They said he was the fastest kid at his age in the United States. I never saw him play, so I didn't believe the hype. Then our coaches brought some game film for us to watch during practice to go over our game plan. My coach that year simply said that to win this game, we would have to stop this kid Damiere Byrd. Then he put the film on. All I'm going to say is there was no hype about Damiere Byrd. It was all real. He really was as fast as they said he was. You know someone is fast when you watch him run and it looks as if he is just jogging but he continues to pull ahead of his opponents on the field. That's how Damiere ran; he made it look so effortless. The craziest part was that he made fast people look slow. That's how I knew this game wouldn't be a walk in the park. But even though we had a tough opponent, we were still going into the game as confident as can be. I mean, the kid was human, just like us.

Finally Friday night came, and we headed to Gloucester Township to play the Stallions. It was a cold night, and it was pouring rain, which made the field conditions horrible. The entire field was covered in mud, and it was tough to get good traction. But that wasn't an excuse, because our opponents had to play in the same conditions. As the game started, I began to feel a pain in my left foot, a nagging pain that would become a sharp, shooting pain at random moments. It made it hard for me to play at my highest level, because I didn't want to put pressure on my foot at all. Heading into halftime, we were down 14–0, and my teammates and I had defeated looks on our faces. It was cold, rainy, and windy, and we just wanted to go home. Well, at least that's how I felt. Plus, the fact that I was injured didn't help my state of mind.

Before we headed back onto the field to finish the second half, a huge thunderstorm came across the area and delayed the game. This didn't help my situation; my injury got even worse. All that time sitting down only made me get tight and aggravated my injury. After we sat in a cold press box for about forty-five minutes, the game finally started back up. I went out to warm up and see whether my injury was any better, but it wasn't. I decided to sit out the rest of the game, because if I had played, I simply would have been a liability to my team. We ended up losing that night 21–7, and Damiere Byrd was responsible for two of his team's touchdowns. We had a sour taste in our mouths after that loss, but we knew we would bounce back and that we were better than that.

The next two games we won, and we finished the season with only one loss on our record. It had been a successful season so far, but we were just getting started, because now we were heading into the playoffs. But guess whom we were playing in the first round. That's right: the Gloucester

Township Stallions and Damiere Byrd. They were the only ones who had beat us in the regular season, but we weren't worried; we were seeking revenge. That entire week of practice, you could see how all my teammates and I were locked in to what our coaches were telling us. The person who really had to pay close attention to the coaches was Courtland, because he had a special job that week. He had to mirror Damiere Byrd all over the field the entire game. Now you know Damiere was fast and one heck of a player, but if there was anybody who was up for the task, it was my big cousin Courtland. So that was the game plan heading into this playoff game. Court literally had the team on his back, and how well he played would determine the outcome of the game.

Game planning is all talk though; we had to show it out on the field. As the game started, right away the Stallions started to feed Damiere the ball in hopes of the usual big play he would create. But it just wasn't happening this time around. Everywhere Damiere went, Court was right in his back pocket. Even though Damiere was faster than Courtland, Court had a great understanding of angles and used that to his advantage. Court had instincts that were very mature for his age, and they showed that day on the field. After four quarters, when there was no time left on the clock, we came out victorious, 42–3, against the Stallions, and we were headed to the next round of the playoffs. Let me just tell you: my cousin Court played his butt off in that game. He did everything he could to make the team successful and then some. For that, Court, thank you. I'll probably never see another performance like that in any level of football. The man literally shut down the fastest kid in the country on every single play, all by himself. If that's not amazing, I don't know what is.

Our next opponents were the Monroe Braves. They were a new team that had just joined our league, but they had tons of talent and were extremely disciplined. I had a connection to the Braves because one of my good friends, Julian Martin, played on the team. Juju, as all his friends called him, played running back for the Braves. I knew Juju because he grew up in Winslow and we played football together. Believe it or not, I had even started to form friendships with other guys from the Braves because I got to know them when I went to Juju's house to visit. Guys like Harry Ulmer and Billy Inge began to know me just as well as they knew Juju. So this game was really about bragging rights among our group of friends, if anything.

Before the game that week, my mom made a bet with me. She said if we won our game against the Braves, we could have a huge pizza party at our house afterward, and the whole team could come. To eleven-year-old me, that sounded like the coolest thing ever. All week during practice, I told my teammates that we had to win this game so we could have this pizza party at my house. I think it got them just as focused as I was, because everyone was super excited when I told them.

Then Saturday came. It was time to show up and show out. As I walked out to the middle of the field for the coin flip, I started laughing because the Braves' captains were all friends of mine. Juju, Harry Ulmer, and Bill Inge shook hands with me before heading back to their sideline. Even though we were all friends, you could tell how serious everyone was; we all wanted to win and were super competitive. As the game got going, it was a completely defensive battle. Eventually, regulation ended in a tie, 7–7.

Now it was time for overtime, and this was for all the marbles. The captains walked back out to the field as the referee explained the rules of overtime. The Braves lost the flip, which gave us control. We decided to go on defense first, so the Braves had the opportunity to score first. Starting from our twenty-five-yard line, the Braves started to drive down the field on us slowly. They got two first downs and were now only five yards away from scoring. On first down from the five, they got no gain. On second down, they tried a passing play, which failed and resulted in a three-yard loss. On third and goal, once again they ran the ball for no gain. Now it was do-or-die time for the Braves. They had one more opportunity to reach the end zone, before we would get our shot at scoring.

My heart was beating out of my chest. I could feel the pressure of the moment in the air. It was a good pressure though. You know those moments you look forward to in your life, but when you're actually in them, you get a little anxious? Well, that was me. All we needed was one more stop, and we were that much closer to having that pizza party at my house. Yup, that's exactly what I was thinking. I wasn't worried about going to the championship; I just wanted some pizza and to hang out with my friends.

Fourth and goal. Juju went into motion, and as the ball was snapped, the quarterback faked the ball to him. All I remember is three guys running toward the end zone, the quarterback rolling out toward them, and no one covering Juju, who was sitting right inside the pylon. The quarterback threw the ball to Juju, and he dropped it. He dropped a for-sure touchdown. I don't know how it happened, I really can't explain it, but it was as if the football gods were looking out for us that day. I looked at Juju, and he seemed so upset about letting his team down. I felt bad for him because he was my friend. But I still had a duty to look out for the best interest of my teammates. I couldn't let them down. I locked back in as it was now our turn to go on offense.

Josh Wilson walked over to the sideline to get the play call from our coach as the rest of us huddled up on the twenty-five-yard line to start our drive. As he came back to the huddle with the play, I was hoping that Coach would call my number and give me the ball. I had one goal in mind, and that was winning. But to be real, I was thinking about that pizza party and how much fun that would be. Josh came back to the huddle with the play, and he said, "Twenty-four power on two."

Now that I look back on it, I can see that what I did next was messed up. I told Josh to change the play and run 43 power. I wasn't trying to be disrespectful to my coach or my teammates. I just had a feeling that if they gave me the ball on this play, I wasn't going to be denied the end zone. Josh looked at me and said, "Are you sure about this?" I just nodded. "Forty-three power on one," Josh said as we broke from the huddle. Remember when I talked about being in the zone in the first chapter? Well, on this play, that's exactly where I was: in the zone. It was as if I had tunnel vision directly to the end zone and no one was in my path. It was only twenty-five yards anyway, right? How hard could it be to get that far and score?

We lined up in our formation, and the ball was hiked. Josh handed the ball off to me as I followed Court and Davon, who were my lead blockers on this play. They did an extraordinary job of clearing a path for me to the end zone. I didn't get touched until I hit the secondary. There in the secondary, I met the safety, who was nicknamed Little Brandon because he was so small. I ran Little Brandon over and just kept moving my legs. Little Brandon held on to my waist, but I was determined to keep pushing toward the goal line. After carrying Little Brandon about seven yards, I saw the end zone. I was only inches away from the goal line as I dove and gave my best effort to score. As I was diving, I felt multiple defenders jump on my back to stop me from scoring. But it was too late. My outstretched arms holding the football crossed the white paint just enough to hear to referee rule touchdown!

We won! We were headed back to the championship. Once I scored, I lay there as my entire team jumped on top of me out of excitement. It was fun at first, and I was happy for us, but then I began to panic. My teammates formed a massive pile, and I was at the bottom of it. Through a small hole in the pile, I could see all the rest of my teammates and coaches running onto the field to join the excitement and most likely jump on me. That's when I really got worried because I started to lose my breath. I couldn't breathe, and I thought I was going to die. Out of pure survival instinct, I started to yell and tell my teammates to get off me because I was suffocating. The fact that I had a helmet on and shoulder pads strapped to my chest didn't help the situation either. But I fought for my life in that moment. I was kicking, punching, and screaming at my teammates to alarm them to get off me. Just as in the AK-47 situation and the brain injury, it just wasn't my time. I don't know how, but I managed to get enough air in my lungs to breathe until all those people finally got off me.

Now my mood was messed up. I was mad at my teammates for almost killing me. I still went over and talked to Juju and all my friends on the other team, but they were short with me, which I understood. If I had been them, I would have been upset as well. Once we parted ways, I looked for Courtland so I could go celebrate with family. When he was in

Willingboro playing football, he never made it to the championship game, because they would always lose in the conference championship. So he had to be excited about this opportunity to finally get there. But he was nowhere to be found. He couldn't have gone already. The game had just ended. I looked over to the sidelines to find Uncle Gawain and Aunt Essy, but I couldn't see them either. Now I started getting worried and thinking about different scenarios in which they would have left, but none of them made sense to me.

People kept giving me hugs as they said congratulations, but I wasn't responsive. I wasn't trying to be disrespectful to them; I just was trying to find my cousin. As the crowd of excited fans dwindled, I found my mom and asked her where Court went. She told me that he had left after we won. That didn't make sense to me. We would always see each other after the game, so this was weird. I headed home with my mom, and during the car ride, my mind was moving a mile a minute. I hoped my cousin was all right and nothing bad had happened to him. At home I asked my dad whether he knew what had happened with Courtland or whether he had seen him leave. My dad said he had seen Uncle Gawain bring my cousin Court off the field, and then they had left. After that, I was clueless about this entire situation.

But don't forget that the whole team still came over to celebrate the victory with the pizza party my mom had promised me if we won. We had a fun time, and everyone was in a great mood. But Courtland was still on my mind. Plus, he didn't come to the pizza party, which really got me wondering what had happened. I mean, who would turn down free pizza?

That weekend I got word that Courtland had quit the team. I forget who told me, but I didn't believe it for the longest time, because I hadn't heard it from my cousin himself. But it bothered me. What had happened? Why? I wanted answers, so I attempted to call Courtland to ask him for the truth, but my mom told me to leave it alone. The fact that she asked me to not call bothered me a lot. I felt she was trying to cover something up. It was only one cousin calling another, so what was the issue? I obeyed my mother's wishes and left it alone. But I could see something was wrong in my parents' body language when I would ask about Courtland. They just got uncomfortable or started acting funny.

Sunday night, I was excited because I would see Courtland the next day at practice as we prepared for the championship game. In my head, all those rumors I was hearing were false. My cousin wasn't going to quit the team. Monday's practice came, but Courtland was nowhere to be found. I didn't understand why. We were winning and having a great time on the field, and we had made it to the championship. The eleven-year-old me did not get it. How could a kid who loved this game so much just up and leave like that? Now all my emotion started to turn on Court, because I felt he was being selfish and letting our team down. We had the most important game of the season ahead of us, and we wouldn't have our best defensive player. And that wasn't the worst part. On top of that, we were playing an undefeated Washington Township Patriots team led by the man himself: Charlie Huff! That's right. We had to face him again, and this time he had an incredible supporting cast around him.

All week during practice, we had to make adjustments not only defensively with the absence of Court but also in the backfield. That entire week I had to play fullback because no one else was better suited to play it. It was a different role for me, but I embraced it because it was what the team needed. After a week of practice, the team headed to Glassboro High School, which hosted that year's championship game. During pregame you could see we didn't look ready to play. I don't want to put it all on Court, but you could tell our teammates knew we needed him to win. It was just a fact; we didn't have all guns on deck.

While we were out at midfield during the coin toss, Charlie Huff had his usual "cooler than the other side of the pillow" look on. So I knew he was ready. I'm going to keep this game brief with you guys and girls: we lost 28–0, and it was worse than the score indicated. They ran up and down the field on us all game, and we couldn't do anything. Offensively, we were a mess and couldn't get anything going at all. That was the season. It ended badly, but we had fun. Well, not in the championship game; that was horrible. Oh yeah, just a sidebar from the story: if anyone ever tells you he had fun losing 28–0 in football at any level, trust me: he's lying. There is nothing fun about that. OK, back to the story.

So now that football was over, my main goal was to figure out what happened with my cousin. For that entire week of practice before the championship game, all my teammates asked me why Courtland had quit. All I could say was "I don't know." That was an honest answer, because I really didn't know, and it bothered me. Some time passed, and Courtland and I hadn't spoken at all. Just to put this in perspective, this is a person I would talk to almost every day, so it was awkward not communicating for a while. Let me be honest as well: our not talking was not just Court's fault. It was equally mine. I wasn't making the effort to reach out to him. I think what was holding me back was the tension between our families that no one wanted to talk about. Why was there tension? I don't know. There just was, and you could feel it at all times.

Then one day I went over to Courtland's house with my mom to talk to him about everything. I was nervous because I didn't know what to expect or how he was going to react. At the same time, though, he was my closest cousin, and if there was anybody I could be real with and talk to, it was him. When I got to his house, I started getting tense and even thought about withholding the questions I was dying to ask him. When I got inside, Aunt Essy was headed out the door past me to go shopping with my mom. So it was just Courtland and I alone at the house with nothing but time to talk.

When I finally saw Court, it was nothing but love. We shook hands and greeted each other as we normally would. After that we headed downstairs to play some video games. I think we played *Madden* or something like that. Then G and Jarret (my other cousins, Courtland's brothers) came home, and we let them play. While they were busy playing *Madden*, Court and I went upstairs. Finally, I had the courage to just say it. "Court, we have to talk about what's going on, because it's bothering me and I feel like there's a lot of tension between us." It felt good to get that off my chest, and it was as if he had been waiting for me to say it the entire time. We went to my aunt and uncle's room. I was thinking, "Why would we have our conversation here?" But then I realized Court and Jarret shared a room, and he didn't want Jarret to interrupt our conversation if he had happened to finish his game early.

I asked Court one simple question: "What happened?" From there he went on to say everything he needed to say. The reason he left after the game was that he felt he wasn't being used enough on offense and wasn't getting a fair shot to play running back. I understood that, since fullback wasn't the most rewarding position in the offense. You were considered more of a lead blocker. Also, Uncle Gawain had a similar mind-set as far as how Court was being used on the offensive side of the ball. With both of them feeling that way, their decision was simple. The only thing I worried about was the vibe I got from Courtland that this decision was more his dad's decision than his. That's what I was still a little unclear about.

After Court and I both got all our words out, it was nothing but love. We shook hands, and for the most part, everything was back to normal. But I will tell you it got a little emotional in there. I don't know why, but it was tough for me to hear what my cousin was saying and how unhappy he was with the team and coaches. He could have said something to me before it got to that. But he didn't, and I understand. That's life.

Just so you know, today Courtland and I couldn't be any closer. We talk all the time about a lot of stuff. We actually recently talked about the situation I just described. Now that I look back on it, I can see that the conversation we had in my uncle and aunt's room probably has enabled us to be honest with each other even to the present day. I feel it was essential to our relationship as family. Now Court, I do want to say to you that I was never mad at you for the decision you made back then. I understand that people make decisions in their lives that they just have to make because it's the right thing for them to do. But I will say, Court, we did need you out on the field that day because none of us could stop Charlie Huff, and you were the man for the job. But that's irrelevant compared to the tension we had. I'm just thankful we got past that and I got my cousin back, and that's all that matters. As far as you, Uncle Gawain, I don't know what your role in that situation was. I just want to let you know I was never mad at you either, or had any hard feelings. However, I do wish I had talked to you about it when I was younger. Now, though, that scenario is so far behind all of us. I'm happy my family is on good terms, and I feel we all learned from that experience, which is most important.

THE PREP

Now that I've covered most of my years as a preteen, let's move into my teenage years. This chapter is "The Prep," and for those who don't know what that refers to, let me tell you a little about it.

At this point in my life, I was in eighth grade, and I was getting ready to make a decision about where I was headed for high school. Most of the people I grew up with were going to be attending our local school, Winslow Township High. That's where I was supposed to go by default, but my parents didn't want me to go there, for numerous reasons. One, they felt I wouldn't be maximizing my opportunity to learn. Two, Winslow High had a reputation for being a little rough and my parents' weren't fans of that. I was already attending Winslow Township Middle School, and it honestly couldn't have been any worse at the high school. But let me just say this before I move on: I love Winslow, and I didn't think there was anything wrong with the education system. At the end of the day, if you apply yourself and lock in to your work, you're going to be successful. Plus, there are life lessons you'll learn in Winslow that you just won't learn other places. At the end of the day, Winslow was in all of us, whether we went to Winslow High School or not. It's just a certain swag or mind-set that was instilled in us and that we will always have.

With that being said, my parents gave me the option to choose from other schools in the area. My parents weren't saying I couldn't go to Winslow High; they just wanted me to have options—that's all. The two options that seemed to stand out from the rest of the pack were Saint Joseph High School, in Hammonton, New Jersey, and Saint Augustine

Prep, in Richland, New Jersey. Both schools had this opportunity called shadowing, which I took advantage of to get a feel for each school. Shadowing is when a prospective student "shadows" or follows a current student around for the day. This enables you to get a feel for the student body, the teachers, and the overall atmosphere of the school. After shadowing at both places, I was a little unsure of where I wanted to attend high school. I had friends from Winslow at both schools, so in an informal way, it was as if they were trying to pitch me and convince me to come to their schools.

The down payment deadline was fast approaching, and I had to make a decision soon. I remember it was a Monday, and my father told me I had to make a decision by Thursday to get the down payment in by Friday. With that on my mind, I was at school all week, weighing the pros and cons of each school. Saint Joe was a powerhouse in football, while the Prep was a basketball school. The Prep was known to offer a far better education than Saint Joe. Saint Joe was fifteen minutes closer to home than the Prep. The Prep had a top-tier wrestling program that for sure could push me in the sport. The biggest difference between the schools was the fact that the Prep was an all-boys school while Saint Joseph was a co-ed school.

After weighing the options, I was still a little unsure of where to go. I asked my parents for their opinions. My dad was 100 percent sold on the Prep. He wanted me to go there so badly. He loved the education provided there, and the fact that they were dominant in wrestling didn't hurt either. I think the icing on the cake for him was the fact that the Prep alumni would refer to their school as a brotherhood, almost like a fraternity of sorts, and because my dad was in a fraternity, he could really connect with that. Now my mother, on the other hand, was very open to both places. She just wanted me to go to the place where I would be the happiest. You know how mothers are.

It was Wednesday, and tomorrow would be the final day I could contemplate my decision. I couldn't focus in school at all. I was worried that I might make the wrong decision, and this was an important one. That entire day I felt Saint Joseph would be a better fit for me. It had a very homey feeling to it, and I was positive that was where I wanted to go to high school. However, I wasn't ready to tell my parents where I wanted to go just yet. I wanted to take advantage of all the time I had. Plus, I wanted to sleep on the fact that I was headed to Saint Joe. If I woke up Thursday morning and it didn't feel right, then I would know the decision was wrong.

But before all that could happen, during dinner on Wednesday night, my dad said something I couldn't believe. He said he had earlier that day paid the down payment for the Prep, so that was where I was going. I was furious! How could he make a decision like that for his child? Well, technically, yes, I get the fact that he could, but why would he do that? He wasn't the one who had to attend the school. Now don't get me wrong. I understood that I was fortunate to have the option to go to the Prep or Saint Joe where others may not have had that option. But that wasn't the point. My dad had just dictated my decision, and it ultimately was a decision I wasn't happy with. I wanted to go to Saint Joe. Remember when I mentioned back in the chapter titled 'The Middle Ages" that my dad forced me to do something one time? Well, this was it.

I was upset for about a week with the decision that had been made for me. I was so salty at my dad for doing that, and for the longest time, I kept our conversations very brief. When he asked me something, I would hit him with one-word answers. I wasn't trying to be rude; I just was frustrated for a little while, and I took it out on him. After a while I cooled off and finally came to the realization that I was going to the Prep. I did ask my dad whether I could still go to Saint Joe, but he said no because he didn't want to lose his money. But really, it was only around $600. I'm not saying that's a little bit of money, but what's more important, your son's happiness or the money?

With only a couple of days at Winslow Middle left, it started to hit me that I was really about to make the switch to the Prep next year. Many people I'd gone to school with my entire life would be gone. Things would be different, but I embraced it because I didn't want to go into the upcoming school year with a negative mind-set. That summer I really lived it up with my friends because this would be the first school year in which I wouldn't be with them. That summer we had so much fun, but it felt as if it flew by.

That summer was cut even shorter because I had summer workouts. It was my first taste of high school football, and it got real for me. It was a rude awakening when I had to run those 110s for the first time. I was so out of shape. I guess it was because I didn't know what to expect when I got there. I was like a chicken with my head cut off. My legs hurt so badly after running those 110s. I just wanted to stop running and sit down. But you have to understand that if you stop running 110s while the rest of the team is still running, it's just not a good look. Whether coaches want to admit it or not, they judge players who don't finish their 110s. And for people who don't know what 110s are, they are 110-yard sprints on the football field. At first they seem bad, but like anything else, once you get used to them, they're easy.

Once school started, I felt I really was in another world. Going to school every day in khakis, a button-up shirt, and a blazer was different for me. At Winslow we could wear whatever we wanted, pretty much. Plus there was the whole fact that it was an all-boys school, but to be honest, once you're there, you get used to it. The biggest adjustment for me was being one of the only black kids in the entire school. At the time there may have been only about twenty of us, and we were all athletes. Every day we would sit at the lunch table together and talk about everything under the sun. It was awkward at first because we were in a lunchroom filled with white kids, and all the brothers sat next to one another at two tables. But you know what? It was like a safe haven to me, to be honest. For that hour at lunch, I was good. I don't know what I mean by "good," but it was just a comfortable feeling.

Now don't get me wrong. I was cool with many of the white boys as well. At a school like that, you have to be. I was always tight with Tom Joyce, whom we'll talk more about later. Then there was my bro Dan Deal, and last but not least was my brother Adam Schroeder. That's right: my old rival/friend was also attending the Prep. It was cool because Adam really bridged the gap for me when it came to meeting new people at the school.

I was cool with the people on the football team, but that was a small population compared to the entire student body.

When I looked around in some of my classes, I didn't see anybody who looked like me. At first it seemed weird, but then I thought, "You know what? This is life." I went through that phase for about the first two weeks; then I got used to it. As the school year progressed, I got more and more settled into the flow of things. When it came to football, I also started to find my role on the team. Now as a freshman, I wasn't the star of the team. I wasn't even playing varsity, to be real. My freshman year, I started JV and freshman, and I played multiple positions. On defense, I played mainly middle linebacker, while on offense I would play running back and fullback. I was OK. I wasn't making any world-class plays or anything like that, but I did give 100 percent effort on every play, and I think that's what made me stand out a little. And when I say "a little," I mean very little. We had a good team that year with some playmakers, especially on the freshman team, so it was tough to shine. So when I had an opportunity, I just had to get mine.

That freshman year we went 6–2 and lost our games to South Jersey powerhouses Holy Spirit and Saint Joe (the other school I was thinking about going to). At the time, those were the big dogs in the Cape Atlantic Conference, and we were on the outside looking in. That year we had some talent on varsity but still fell short of both teams when it came time to put the pads on.

At this point, football season was over, and I was bummed about that. I had started to get a taste of higher levels of competition and wanted to keep playing, but there was always next year; I just had to wait. The next thing for me was wrestling season. I never told my pops this, but I was so checked out of the sport of wrestling by the time I got to high school. I didn't have a care in the world about wrestling anymore. I wrestled so much in little league that I was burnt out. But I didn't tell him I didn't want to wrestle in high school, and he was 100 percent sure I did. He would ask me whether I wanted to wrestle in high school, and I would say yes. Looking back on it, I don't know why I didn't tell him the truth. Shoot, it would have saved me a whole bunch of BS, time, and unnecessary exhaustion. I think the reason I was lying to not only him but also myself was to make him happy. This was the last straw for the sport of wrestling in our family. I mean, he coached me all those years and put in all that time with me, and I truly believe he wanted to see me blossom at the high school level. You know how parents are; they're all proud of you after sporting events, especially when you succeed. What parent wouldn't want to see his or her child succeed? But for my pops, it was bigger than that—well, at least in my head it was. So I really did it for him, to make him happy. For the young kids who are reading this, please don't ever sacrifice your happiness for someone else's. Now if you have a child, that's a completely different situation that I'm not knowledgeable about, but you know what I mean.

As I said earlier, the Prep was a dominant wrestling team in the area and had a reputation of success. Coach Keith Hoover led us, and he was a somewhat-intimidating person. Not that you would be afraid of him, but he had a mustache and a certain look he would give you that made you stand up straight. I think that going into the season, some of my teammates had high expectations for me. Some of it may have come from hearing about my prior success as a youngster through the grapevine. The other half may have been from me. I've never shared this with anybody, but here it is: at fourteen I didn't have a great understanding of boasting and the negative effects it can have on you if you don't live up to expectations. Now I'm not going to lie to you or myself. My soon-to-be teammates would ask me about my success when I was younger, and I would proudly tell them. But what I didn't get back then was that not only was all that prior success irrelevant at that level but also I was building up expectations that I could never fulfill. I was young, and I was stupid, but I'll tell you what: I'm happy I learned my lesson.

It all started the day after Thanksgiving. They called it Hell Week at the Prep. It was three days of mental and physical fatigue. It was definitely the hardest three days of my life up to that point. That first day we got there, we started running at seven in the morning. The first thing we had to do was run thirteen miles. When we were done, we all met on the football field at the back of the school. Next we did numerous fifty-yard suicides, then fifty-yard sprints, followed up by four corners. For those who don't know what these different exercises are, don't worry; just know I was extremely tired. Not only were our coaches trying to get all that food from Thanksgiving out of our systems by making us throw up, but they also were trying to weed out the people who were quitters. Even though I didn't want to wrestle, I wasn't a quitter, and I'm not now. After a couple more running exercises and about ten more people on the team throwing up, we headed into the weight room to start lifting. Now that was more my element. Running I wasn't the biggest fan of, but weights I had no problem with. I just knew it wasn't running, so it was cool with me.

After lifting, we headed into the gym to start practice. Now just in case I didn't cover it earlier, I want you to understand that the last time I was seriously wrestling was my sixth-grade year in middle school. In seventh grade I did it here and there for my middle school team when I wanted to, and in eighth grade I thought I was going to the NBA, so I didn't wrestle at all. Mind you, all those guys whom I used to wrestle against when I was younger were still wrestling year-round and getting better, while I had hoop dreams. So now, as I bring you back to the first practice we had on the first day of Hell Week, I want to paint a clear picture.

To keep a long story short, I was rusty! Matter of fact, "rusty" isn't even the word. When I was out there on the mat I was just bad. I just didn't have it anymore. Not only did I not want to be there, but that "it" factor I had when I was younger was gone. The moment I knew I wasn't the same was when we started live wrestling in practice against our teammates. It sounds as if it fits into the story perfectly, but Schroeder and I were back at it, battling on the mat again. We were the same weight class again, and we would have to compete against each other for the starting spot on the team. That was just reality. When we did live wrestling for the first time in practice against each other, right away I knew he was light-years ahead of me. It was one of the most humbling moments of my life, and I'll never forget it. It showed me that if you keep working at something, eventually you'll get better, and Adam was proof of that.

I couldn't beat Adam to save my life if it came down to that. He was faster, stronger, quicker, and definitely more knowledgeable of the sport than I was. Every time we'd live wrestle each other, I'd think to myself that I felt bad for him; I felt I was wasting his time. It was that bad. I was no competition for him, simply because of the gap in our skill levels. I even remember Adam telling me to stop playing around and really wrestle him, almost as if he knew that the old me was still in there. But it wasn't; it was completely gone. Adam, I want to say sorry for wasting your time. I apologize for that, because you were there trying to get better and work, and I wasn't much help.

Once the season got started, I was wrestling on the JV team, and that's where I deserved to be. That sounds sad, but it's true. My first match that year was at a school in North Jersey. I forget the name of the school; I just remember it being far away and cold that day. My first match I won by pinning the guy within the first couple of seconds of the second period. Don't get me wrong; even though I wasn't starting over Schroeder, all that practice did make me better. I wasn't the old me, but I wasn't horrible either. I got a little confidence after getting my first win at the high school level under my belt, even though it was JV. My coaches told me that my next match that day was against a solid opponent, but I didn't know the kid, so I didn't care. The match started out slow as both of us stalled for the first thirty seconds. Neither one of us was being the aggressor. We even got stalling calls called on both of us within the first thirty seconds of the match, which is rare. After the stalling call, I chose to be the aggressor and take my shot at a possible double-leg takedown.

The attempt failed, but when I got back up on two feet, I inelegantly fell back down to the mat. It was weird; when I took my shot, I felt the smallest pinch in my left hamstring. I thought nothing of it because it felt so minor, but when I tried to stand back up after falling to the ground, I fell again. I didn't understand; I didn't feel any pain in my leg. Then I grabbed my hamstring, and I felt a huge knot at the top of my leg, right below my butt. It was huge, and once I felt the knot, all the pain hit me immediately. It was as if a delayed shock wave of pain hit me. The most random part about the entire situation was the fact that my opponent was just looking at me in disbelief as I was falling to the ground. He was in shock when I couldn't stand on my own two feet. Let's just say I was as surprised at what happened as he was.

The final verdict was that I had partially torn my left hamstring. That was the end of my wrestling career. On the long ride back down to South Jersey, I had a lot of time to think about the whole situation. The bad part was I had really messed my hamstring up and I was going to be out of commission for a while. To me, the good part was that in my head, I was done with the sport of wrestling. It sounds bad for me to have gone out like that, but that's life. I can't pick and choose when I'm going to get injured.

The next couple of months were a gift and a curse. Treatment on my messed-up hamstring lasted for months, but I got through it. I was happy that I was done with wrestling, but there was a catch. As I said earlier, I wasn't a quitter. So for the rest of the year, I traveled with the team to different high schools in South Jersey to support them. Now, did I want to be there? No, not at all, and I really could've used that time to study, which I needed to do more. The worst part of it all was that people on the team started treating me with disrespect. Sometimes they would make racist comments toward me or tell me to do little chores for them before matches since I wasn't wrestling. I used to snap back, and trust me: I wanted to throw the hands multiple times. But I had a partially torn hamstring, so I wasn't moving too well. I was in a vulnerable state. I think some of the hate toward me came from the expectations everyone had for me prior to the season starting, which I had added to. They probably thought I was a liar and this was their way of getting back at me. I'm not saying what they did was right, but I can see how everything that happened could have made them think I was a liar. And we all know no one likes liars. I never told my parents, my coaches, or even my friends, because by that point, I had already made the decision to transfer. I knew the Prep wasn't the place for me. So in a very sarcastic way, I'm going to say thanks, Dad, for sending me there.

You know what, though? I really do appreciate all the things I went through during that wrestling season. I learned a lot, believe it or not. I learned that I could push myself physically and mentally a lot further than I thought I could. It taught me to be humble. It taught me so much discipline. The injury taught me that at any moment your health can be taken away from you, so whatever you're doing, do it at a hundred miles per hour. Finally, that wrestling season taught me that there is still hate in this world and that you need to be picky about the vibes and energy you surround yourself with, because you owe yourself that much.

I feel I needed this chapter in my life for so many reasons. There are probably reasons I won't even understand until I'm a little older, but in time, those experiences will come in handy. Now, I do want to state that I enjoyed the Prep. I loved the teachers, and they were always very helpful. The facilities at the Prep were second to none in the South Jersey area, when it came to not only the classroom but also the playing fields. As far as the food goes, it was excellent. My favorite part of the day was always breakfast and lunch. Chef Paul would have those cookies going, and the entire building would smell like heaven. Seriously though, the school was awesome, but it just wasn't the right fit for me, and I knew it.

As my freshman year was ending, I finally popped the question to my parents about transferring. I could tell my mom was so happy, because she could tell how unhappy I was at the Prep. My dad was another story. At first, he gave me reasons why I should stay at the Prep, but eventually he realized that my mind was already made up. So he stopped wasting his breath and finally accepted that I wanted to go to Saint Joseph.

One day after school at the Prep, there was a huge basketball game. It was Saint Joseph versus the Prep. That day, my mom came to pick me up from school after the game. She came a little early and happened to get to the school around halftime. Since we had a little time before the game started again, I gave her a little tour of where some of my classes were. While I was showing Mom around, we ran into two girls in the hallway. They stopped my mom and I and asked me if my name was Gordon Hill. They were wearing hoodies with "Saint Joseph's" printed across the torso.

I said yes, and they said they heard I might be transferring to Saint Joe soon. It was weird. I didn't know these girls, but they seemed to know a lot about me and my intent to transfer. I did have a good number of friends from Sicklerville who went to Saint Joe whom I talked to and told I might be transferring there. That had to be how they knew. As the conversation continued, they confirmed that was exactly how they found out.

My mom was interested in hearing their perspectives on Saint Joe, and they were selling it as if it was the greatest place on earth. I was happy about that though, because as long as my mom is happy, I'm happy, and vice versa. If anyone was wondering, Saint Joe pulled off one of the biggest upsets in South Jersey basketball history that night. Norman White put Saint Joe on his back and led them to victory against a team they were definitely supposed to lose to.

A couple of days later, after I made my decision to transfer, I told some of the guys from the Prep I had become cool with. Ironically, one of them, my bro Tom Joyce, said he was thinking about transferring to Saint Joe too, but I didn't believe him at all. I thought he was just playing with me to be funny, but after a while I started to believe him. We would talk to each other about the future and how different the next year was going to be at a different school. You could tell we were both ready to move on.

Finally, finals week hit, and I was more than ready to be done with them. I don't remember all the finals I had that year, but I do remember my last one. It was in bio, and it was upstairs in the new building. Bio was my favorite class that year. I was confident I was going to do well because I knew all the material. When I finished the test, I knew I aced it. After the test that day, I had a couple of hours to burn before the buses brought everyone home. There was a big group of kids outside of the new building playing cee-lo on a table. If you don't know what cee-lo is, it's a dice game using three dice where people bet money on each roll. The goal is simply to roll the highest number. After watching a couple of rounds, I decided to play one last game before I left this school for good. It was a $5 buy-in, and seven other people bought in for that round. I was second to roll, and I rolled a strong five. I was confident no one else would roll anything higher, but with cee-lo, you never know, because it's a game of luck. On that day, luck must have been on my side, because I walked away from that table $35 richer. Not only that, but when I got home, I found out I got a ninety-two on my bio exam.

Later that day, I got a call from my former head football coach at the Prep, Coach Dennis Scuderi. Word had got around to him that I was transferring to Saint Joseph and that I wouldn't be returning next season. He asked me why I had transferred, and I told him the school just wasn't for me. What he said to me next has stuck with me forever. He told me that I would never play at Saint Joseph. I don't know why you would tell a fifteen-year-old kid that, but I want to say thank you for doubting me, Mr. Scuderi, because I used your comments as motivation for the next couple of years.

Welcome to Saint Joe Football

Sophomore year was an interesting time in my life. Obviously it was a big transition because I transferred schools. I was in a totally different atmosphere and around all these brand-new faces and personalities. I had new teammates and a brand-new coaching staff who didn't know a thing about me. I was extremely happy with my decision to transfer, and I was 100 percent committed to my decision. I looked forward to all the new experiences and the people I would meet on the way.

The first encounter I had with my new teammates was at the annual Saint Joseph Football Dead-a-Thon, a fundraiser where players lifted weights for contributions. It took place in May every year, and it was a great way for me to get to know some of the guys before we hit the field in the summer. As I said earlier, I already knew some people on the team from my hometown of Sicklerville. Guys like Phil Paulhill, Todd Bockarie, and Drew Terry I had known since I was little, and they made the transition a little bit smoother for me. They treated me like family and introduced me to the rest of the team. There was another familiar face at the Dead-a-Thon that night as well: Tom Joyce from the Prep. He had told me he was transferring to Saint Joe, but I couldn't believe it until I saw it with my own eyes. Tom was always the class clown, and he would joke around a lot, so I never knew when to take him seriously. This time, he was serious. Overall, it was a great introduction to the program. The team seemed very close and about their business, which I liked a lot. Now I just had to find my role on the team.

I mentioned it briefly earlier, but Saint Joe was known as one of the best, if not the best, football team in South Jersey year in and year out. When I transferred there, they were coming off one of their down years. However, prior to the previous year, they had a streak of eight straight state-championship titles. Saint Joseph has the most state championships in New Jersey football history, and Coach Sacco has one of the highest amounts of wins in the state.

Now, before the question even pops into your head, I didn't go to Saint Joe for football alone. Did I know they were successful in the sport? For sure I did, but that wasn't the main reason at all. I simply went there because I felt it would be a better fit for me. Just so you know, Saint Joe wasn't too different from the Prep as far as demographics. The student body was majority Caucasian, just like the Prep, along with the staff. But Saint Joe was a lot smaller, and I had at least three to four teammates in every class. I just wanted to let you know so you could paint a better picture.

Now, let me take you to the summertime grind of Saint Joe football and the infamous field house. The field house, weight room, or whatever you want to call it was like the heartbeat of Saint Joe football. That's where everything got done, pretty much. We lifted there and watched film; it used to serve as our athletic training room as well. Everything went on at the field house. But if the field house was the heartbeat of our program, then Coach Paul Sacco Jr. was the nucleus of it all. He's a five-foot-two Italian man from Hammonton, New Jersey. But don't let his height fool you; he's a passionate powerlifter, a spontaneous comedian, and one hell of a football coach.

In the summertime, the entire team would come to the field house to get a lift in three days a week, and Coach Sacco would monitor our every move. He would be tough on us because he wanted us to be as prepared as possible when the season came around. Now, Saint Joe football may not have always had the best athletes in the area, but Coach made sure we were stronger than everyone else. So when it came to the weight room and our lifts, he took it very seriously. When I first started lifting with the team, Coach was always in my ear, making sure I got all my lifting in each day.

He would walk into a room full of twenty people and make a comment to me only. He'd make a joke like, "Gordon, you only have two hundred five pounds on the bar? My mom did that this morning, and she's eighty years old." That's what I had to deal with for the longest time, but I got used to it. It was Coach's way of connecting with some of the players while also motivating us. At first it got on my nerves because I thought he was being hard on me for no reason. Then I thought he was doing it because I came from a rival school and he wanted to joke about it a little. But then I realized he actually did it to everybody, no matter who you were. Plus, I started to understand that it was good for coaches to always be on you about the little things.

To all the young kids who may read this book, please understand what I'm about to say next. When a coach is being tough on you or is always on your case or on your back, it is actually a great sign; it tells you that the coach cares about you and is willing to devote his or her time to be critical of your mistakes. In the end, this will be beneficial to you because it will make you a better player. So don't get frustrated when a coach is yelling at you about doing the little things the right way. It just shows that he or she cares. Now if a coach isn't yelling at you or isn't correcting your mistakes, then that's a bad sign. At that point you should be worried, because it shows that the coach has given up on you as a player and doesn't care about your success and you fulfilling your potential. My advice in this scenario is to talk to your coach one-on-one and figure out why you two have some type of disconnect. All right, back to the story.

Another thing Coach started to do was call me Goose. The name came about one week during summer lifting. Every time Coach walked by me during lifting, I would be in between sets. While taking a short break, I would talk to my new teammates to get to know them a little better. Coach, for some reason, would always see me talking and never lifting. So from that week on, he named me Goose after Mother Goose because he said I was always telling someone a story. Now that I wrote this book, I think it's ironic he gave me that nickname all the way back then. I guess he was onto something. Although Coach and my teammates got a laugh out of it, it didn't bother me. I was the new kid on the block, so it came with the territory. Besides, I knew that once they saw me play, all those jokes and nicknames would eventually fade away.

Camp started, and I finally got a chance to show them what I was capable of. During the first couple of days, I was a little behind everyone else because they knew the playbook and how things were done around here. So I just had to keep my head down, my mouth shut, and my ears and eyes open. I was trying to grasp everything I could as fast as I could so I would gain the coaches' trust ASAP. Little by little I started to understand the playbook and what the coaches' expectations were. I have introduced only Coach Sacco so far, but we did have other coaches, and trust me: they all brought their own personalities to the coaching staff. We had Coach Stalba, who was the running backs / linebackers coach, and he was crazy. The man was just out of his mind, but in a good way. He'd do backflips, run into players without pads on, and always bring an endless amount of energy to practice. Then we had the WRs coach, Coach Roberts, who seemed to be the most level headed. Then we had Coach Curcio, who was just the man; he was definitely a player's coach. If you ever needed to talk to a coach, he was the one to go to. Finally, we had Coach Rick Mueriello, the biggest character of them all. Coach Rick played so many roles as a coach. He could be the nice guy, the intimidating coach, the players' coach, or the guru; sometimes, when his kids were around us at practice, he would turn into a dad. He was an interesting fellow; let's just leave it at that. Regardless of what I'm saying, you really had to meet all of them because they were all fun to be around, especially when they were all together. All right, so now that I have them covered, let me get back into the story.

As camp progressed, I started to adjust to everything. I started to get comfortable enough to be myself out there on the field and not think so much. To all my football players out there, you know what I'm talking about. At this point I had to prove myself not only to my coaches and my teammates but also to myself. I had to show myself that I had what it took to be a starter on this team. Coming from a rival team and playing only freshman and JV the year prior didn't give me the best credentials, so I had to earn my right to play. At running back, I was third string behind a stable of running backs. I was the youngest one and the newest to the team, but I didn't care, because I knew I was better than all of them. I'm not trying to sound cocky; I was just confident in my ability and knew I could bring something different to this backfield. That year the guys who started running back were Jarred Bianchini, Ashton Alicea, John Barillo, and Nick Haines. They were all good players, and I learned something from all of them by watching, but I felt it was my time. I was ready, but Coach Sacco had other plans.

I knew my best chance to prove that I should get an opportunity to be a starter at running back was by shining on the scout team. Every time the scout team went up against the first defense, I would jump up to get a chance to run the ball. Every chance I got, I tried to score a touchdown on the first-team defense to prove I belonged as a starting running back. One day, I was at scout-team running back, and the play called in the huddle was 929 sweep on set. I got in formation as I prepared to receive the ball. The ball was hiked and handed off to me. I followed my blockers and then looked back for a potential cutback lane that looked promising. I cut the run back in to what I thought was a cutback lane, but I was wrong. As soon as I got to the hole, the biggest defensive lineman on the team, Eddie Harper, met me. He bear-hugged me and slammed me down to the ground. As he was getting up from the ground, he looked me dead in the eye and said, "Welcome to Saint Joe football." That was my eye-opening welcome into the program. It showed me that I wouldn't be able to get away with the things I did in little league. It showed me I had some maturing to do both physically and mentally as a player.

Not only was starting at running back one of my objectives, but I also wanted to start on defense at safety. So every day, in between my running back reps, I would go out and play as a WR. Every time I ran a route, I intentionally tried to embarrass the defensive backs who were out there. It was nothing personal; I just had to show Coach Sacco that maybe a change should be made. When I ran my routes, I'd put in as much effort as I had in me to make a great play on the ball. Over the duration of a couple of practices, Coach Sacco started to notice how badly I dismantled the defensive backfield. He would make comments to them like, "I don't know, guys. The way Gordon is killing you, we may lose every game by forty points this year." At that point, I knew I had his attention. Now all I had to do was make some plays out there in practice when I was at DB.

Now, I'd made my fair share of plays at either corner or safety, but I didn't think I made enough for Coach to make a change. That was on me; that was my fault. The season was getting started, and I didn't seem to crack the starting lineup on either defense or offense, but I didn't let it bother me. Was I disappointed a tiny bit? Yeah, of course, because I knew I could help better the team, but that's life. Sometimes things don't go your way. I kept working though. The first game I played as a Saint Joe Wildcat was on Tuesday in the JV game against Bridgeton High School at home. I was excited, of course, for the opportunity to play ball, but I took it as disrespect because the coaches still didn't believe I could play varsity. So I had to show them I deserved to play in the prime time.

That first JV game against Bridgeton, I had two touchdowns and about 175 yards rushing on maybe ten or twelve carries. Defensively, I had a couple of tackles and two interceptions, and at kick returner I almost ran back two kick returns. I had a field day, and it wasn't for me or because I was mad at Bridgeton or anything like that. I did it to prove to the coaches that I was ready for the big time. The varsity won week 1, but I didn't play in the varsity game at all. News about my performance spread. Remember I had just transferred in from a rival school, so I had a whole lot to prove, mainly to myself. Because yes, the coaches may have had expectations for me, but I always have higher expectations for myself. I'm definitely my biggest critic when it comes to my performance.

Our next opponent was Middle Township, and no disrespect to them, but they were a warm-up game. That week of practice, it occurred to me that it could be my time to get in late in this week's game if we extended the lead early enough. But I wasn't looking for garbage time; I just saw it as an opportunity. That entire week of practice, I could see how people were treating me a little differently. I had earned a couple of my teammates' respect. They finally realized I could ball. During practice, I would stick to my game plan of going all out against the first-team defense or offense depending on what side of the ball I was on. Even though I was starting to get cool with the guys on the team, when it came to football practice, that was business. I wasn't your friend; I was trying to take your job. Straight up! It was nothing personal. I was doing what I had to do to become a varsity starter.

See, when I was six years old, watching Mike Vick on Saturdays, my mother had explained to me this thing called a scholarship. She explained what it was and how it would make my life easier down the road. She told me I had to do well in football and, more importantly, in school. It seemed like an easy task to me. I just knew I had to start on my high school team for this to come to fruition. So that's what I was doing: trying to make my life easier with a scholarship. It just so happened that Allen McMurren, Matt McGlynn, Nick Haines, Austin Regalbuto, and Jarred Bianchini were in the way of that. They were the starting defensive backs. I didn't care whose job I took; I just knew it had to be someone's.

Finally it was game time, and I was excited about this one because Coach Sacco said I would be playing a little at corner. He even told me not to play that much in the JV game that week in preparation for this game. I guess he really wanted to see what I had. Middle Township had a couple of speedy wide receivers that year, so I knew I would be tested on the deep ball, for sure. When the game started, I was a little nervous. It would be my first real action in a varsity game, and although I was nervous, I was also extremely excited. The first drive defensively, Coach sent out the usual starting DBs (defensive backs). I was waiting my turn on the sideline; I didn't know what his intentions were as far as putting me in the game. The next time we were on defense, Coach Sacco said I was up at cornerback.

This was it: my time to shine. I stepped out on the field with the rest of the defense and locked in. The first play I was out there, I was lined up across from the fastest WR (wide receiver) on the other team. The ball was hiked, and the WR ran as fast as he could toward me. I knew they were going to try to take a shot at the end zone against me, since I was the new guy. I could tell he was going deep by the way he released off the line. So I flipped my hips and ran in sync with him down the field as I turned my head to find the ball. It was a bomb; the QB probably threw the ball fifty yards in the air, and neither one of us could catch up to it. It was an incomplete pass. They probably thought this five-foot-eight sophomore with no gloves on was trash. They weren't wrong for thinking that though. I would have taken a shot against me as well if I were them.

The remainder of the game, Jarred Bianchini and I flip-flopped at corner every series. The rest of the game, I wasn't challenged by any passes, but I did get in on a couple of tackles, which was great for my confidence. Football is like anything in life; the more reps you do, the more comfortable you get. We won that game 35–6, but this was just the beginning for me.

The next week we were matched up against Pleasantville, and they always had a couple of athletes on their team. Early in the week, Coach Sacco told me that I was starting at corner, so I had to be ready. During that week in class, I'd constantly think about the game and envision myself making a big play, even getting a pick six or something like that. During practice, the coaches really pushed me to the limit all week in preparation for my first start. They would call pass plays in my direction intentionally just to see how I would react in different scenarios. I was ready though; I was just waiting for game time.

Friday night finally rolled around, and we headed to Pleasantville. I was a little nervous, as usual. All my teammates kept asking me whether I was ready to play, and I would calmly say yes. When the game started and I locked in to my assignments, nothing else in the world mattered. I wasn't worried about anything but the man across from me. Early on, Pleasantville tried to go deep on me, but I was in good coverage. Then they tried quick game against me, some slants and comebacks just to get the QB in rhythm, but that didn't work either. Now, I wasn't that confident at DB yet, and I especially wasn't that comfortable at corner. So it's not that I was locking up the WRs. I was able to get the job done though, especially at the high school level. What helped me was a couple of dropped balls, an overthrow, bad timing, and constant pressure from my front seven. As I look back, I realize the coverage could have been better. It was my first start. But as you can see, I'm still hard on myself regarding my performance.

With an insurmountable lead heading into the fourth quarter, Pleasantville continued to take deep shots down the field. This was my chance to get an interception, and I knew it. I just had to be prepared when the opportunity came. Pass after pass continued not to go my way, until finally I got a shot. The QB dropped back, and the WR ran directly toward me. I was in perfect position, as I knew they were going to run a fly route. The QB released the ball as I turned my hips to run with the WR, but as he threw it, he was hit by one of my teammates. Now the ball was just a floating duck in the air, and the only person who could get to it was me. The WR didn't know it was an underthrown ball, because he still didn't have his eyes turned around. So I planted my foot and headed back toward the line of scrimmage to get my first high school varsity pick. As the ball got closer and closer to my hands, I noticed that there wasn't a Pleasantville player in sight. Once I caught this, I was going to score a touchdown for sure, and then…I dropped it! A for-sure interception touchdown went directly through my hands and hit me in my face. Yup, it's true. I can blame it on so many things: the lights, the fact that I didn't have any gloves on, or whatever the case may have been. But really, I didn't have an excuse. I just dropped it. I got a little too excited about the opportunity to make such a big play. My eyes got huge when I saw the end zone and no one in sight. I learned my lesson though: catch the ball first before you try to run. Also, it was good for me to get the excitement of a big play out of my system so I wouldn't be so jittery the next time. I would call a moment like that a growing pain as a player. We all go through them eventually.

After the dropped interception, my teammates got a laugh out of it and then encouraged me to be ready for the next one. We left Pleasantville with a 40–0 victory that night, but we knew tougher opponents were ahead of us.

The next week, we were playing Holy Spirit. Now, Holy Spirit is 1,000 percent one of our rivals at Saint Joe. You can lose almost every game (not really), but as long as you beat Holy Spirit and a couple of other teams, that's all that matters. When Saint Joe and Holy Spirit are matched up, it's the biggest event going on in the state that night. That's the magnitude of our matchups. There were so many different nicknames for the game, but the one I always liked best was the Holy War. That year we both were headed into the game undefeated at 3–0. We were two heavyweight champs matched up against each other; we just had to see who would prevail.

I'm not even going to mention practice that week. Just know it was real and the coaches were on us about everything. Let's just get to the game.

As we pulled into the school, we were greeted as a rival should be. A whole bunch of profanities and multiple evil stares were thrown in our direction. When we got in the locker room, I was super nervous. I could feel the energy of the moment and how important this game was to so many people. Before we left to head to the field, my bro Todd Bockarie asked me whether I was nervous. I lied to him and said, "A little," knowing I was terrified. It wasn't that I was scared of the moment, but I was always nervous because I didn't want to let my teammates down.

We left the locker room and headed down to the field. Our coaches were so jacked up for the game it was ridiculous. Right before I made my way onto the field, Coach Mueriello punched the top of my shoulder pads to get me going for the game. That killed my right shoulder. I got a stinging sensation that went all the way down my arm. I started to panic because I thought he really injured me. Then my right arm went numb for a couple of seconds. Eventually it all went back to normal, but it scared me because I thought I might have dislocated my shoulder or something. So Coach Mueriello, please stop hitting kids on top of their shoulder pads before games, because you just might hurt them. Especially before the Holy Spirit game, because I know how amped up you get for those.

Before the first kickoff, the crowd was roaring! This was the biggest game I'd ever been in and the largest amount of people I'd ever played in front of. When we finally got on defense, I knew I'd be matched up against a six-foot-two WR named Jason Smart-El. He had a decent height advantage over me, so I knew they were going to try me on a couple of jump ball plays. I wasn't worried about it though; I was looking forward to the challenge.

Leading up to the last couple of minutes before halftime, the score was tied 0–0. It was a stalemate. Spirit still had the ball with about two minutes left before halftime, and I knew they were going to take a shot at the end zone. It was third down and about seven to go. The ball was hiked, and I saw the QB look immediately in my direction. The ball was coming, and I knew it. I located my WR and then looked into the air, as I was in perfect position to make a play on the ball. I jumped up with my heels on the goal line in preparation for another sure interception like the prior week. Then, out of nowhere, Jason Smart-El came from behind me and snagged the ball away from me. I had jumped too early. I got mossed in front of thousands of people. Two weeks in a row, I had missed my opportunity to make a big play for my team, and I let them down again. But this time, we weren't up by thirty-two points with only a couple of minutes left in the game. We were down 7–0 about to head into halftime. After the play, my pride was hurt. Like, really hurt. I knew right away it was going to look bad on the film the next day. But my teammates came over to me and reminded me that we still had another half to play and they needed me out there. So I would have to let this one go and forget about it.

Seconds after the TD, I just let up. On the ensuing kickoff, my teammate Austin Regalbuto ran back an eighty-yard kick return for a touchdown. The game was now tied 7–7 going into halftime. After Austin ran back that kick return, I felt so much better because the score was basically back to 0–0. It was as if the touchdown I had just let up never happened. Well, at least that's how I justified it in my head. So thank you, Austin, for making a big play, because not only did we need it as a team but also I needed it for my confidence.

The remainder of the game I played decently, but we ended up losing after Holy Spirit scored with five minutes left in the game. The final score was 13–9. The next day I came into the field house, and the first thing I saw was the cover of the *Atlantic City Press*. It had a picture of me getting mossed by Jason Smart-El in the end zone. If my confidence and pride weren't already shaken up after that game, they were now. I was so embarrassed, and it didn't help that some of my teammates were laughing at me about it. They weren't trying to be malicious. It was more like a "Come on, G. You can't let this happen to you again" type of laugh. But they were right; I couldn't let something like that happen again. Not only had I let my team down, but I had also let my family down. My last name was printed in the paper under that picture, and I wasn't proud of that at all. Most importantly though, I had let myself down, and there was no one but myself to blame for me being in that situation. I should've made a play on the ball, and if I had, none of this would have been happening right now. None of these feelings would've come about, and we probably would have even won the game if I hadn't let up that touchdown. As you can see, this bothered me for a while.

I do want to say thank you to Jason Smart-El for mossing me that night. I needed that so much, because that picture on the cover of the *Atlantic City Press* motivated me to work harder to ensure nothing like that would ever happen again. I want to thank the *Atlantic City Press* for putting that picture on the cover of the sports page the next day. To the person who took the picture, not only is it a great shot, but it was also my motivation for the next couple of years. So thank you, thank you so much. I needed that.

For the rest of the year, I played my heart out and got better and better every game. As a team, we had one of the worst years in Saint Joe history. We went 5–5 and just weren't competitive enough. That year is what we needed though. In fact, that sophomore year was exactly what I needed. I needed those bumps, bruises, and moments when I failed, because I knew they would only make me stronger as a person and player, and they did.

Tough Love

Junior year of football was about to begin, and many key guys were coming back. In my class alone, we had Phil Paulhill (CB, WR), Pat Casey (TE, LB), Josh Moore (LB, OL), Nick O'Brien (OL, DL), Mike Mazzeo (OL, DL), Todd Bockarie (WR, K), and me all returning. This was the first year in which we all were going to be two-way starters. At Saint Joe, we didn't have the numbers that public schools had, which allowed them to play their guys on only one side of the ball. It wasn't like that at Saint Joe, and I don't think Coach Sacco believed in that either. He just kept the best eleven on the field for each scenario. So what we learned over time was how not to get tired. We couldn't get fatigued; we just played through it and gave what we had left on every play.

I'd be lying if I told you I was prepared going into camp that year, because I wasn't. Some days I'd be so tired, but I wouldn't say anything to Coach, because I already knew what he would have said. Plus, I had acquired the starting running back position and didn't want to show him I wasn't ready for the extra workload. There also was the constant reminder that a number of RBs behind me would have killed for the opportunity I had. So I had to suck it up and keep working. I mean, my goal was to get a scholarship, right? The way I looked at it, playing both sides of the ball gave me more opportunities to make plays.

Throughout the weeks prior to our first game against Bridgeton, I really analyzed our team as a whole during practice. When we got break time in between drills, I would sit there and think about a lot of things. For example, I would think about who was serious about the game, or whom I could rely on when times got tough on the field, or whom we could go to for a big play when we needed it. Now looking back on that year, I realize I should have been asking some of those same questions about myself. I mean, I could deliver a big play here or there, but I wasn't where I needed to be physically or mentally to help the team maximize its ability to win. I was complacent and comfortable where I was. I was comfortable with starting at RB; I enjoyed the title of "starting RB." I'm not saying I didn't work hard for it, because I did, but I could have pushed myself a lot harder when it came down to preparation before the season. That's where I let myself down, as well as my team.

It was as if I was consciously lying to myself, trying to convince myself that I was prepared when I knew I wasn't ready for that season's demands. This wasn't something that was just going on in my head; it was something you could see for yourself. If you look back at highlights of my junior year, you can see how slow I was. I mean, I had a first gear, and I could get into second, but I wouldn't stay there long. I couldn't hold my top-end speed, and it showed when I got hawked (caught from behind) by multiple defenders that year. Remember when I talked about being in the zone in chapter 1? It was as if I couldn't get back to that place anymore, and it was a disheartening feeling.

Finally, the first game was here, and we were matched up with the Bridgeton Bulldogs. Saint Joe hadn't lost to Bridgeton since 1989, and we weren't planning to break the streak. But we did on that cold, rainy Friday night down in Bridgeton. We lost 14–6, and as a team, we were in shock. We really underestimated them that year. Don't get me wrong; that year they were extremely talented on both sides of the ball, but also we didn't play our best. I had the only TD that night, but it wasn't about individual stats or me. I just wanted to figure out how we could get this thing going in the right direction; I didn't want another 5–5 season like the previous one.

After the loss, not only were my teammates mad, but we could tell Coach Sacco was just as frustrated. When I looked at him, it almost seemed as if he had given up on us already, or as if he didn't care anymore. Remember that this was a man who had been doing this for years, so to see him like that was unusual. This was the first game of the season, so I knew he'd get through it. It was just a tough loss for everyone.

After that loss, we all had to look ourselves in the mirror and be honest with ourselves. Were we really who we thought we were? Were we a team that could win another state championship, or was that wishful thinking? See, I truly believe that when you go to Saint Joseph High School and you decide to play football, you get caught up in the tradition. All you ever hear about playing there is winning. You end up just assuming you will win. What those unsuccessful teams at Saint Joe didn't understand was that you still have to put in the work and perform on game day. Just because you have the name Saint Joseph on the front of your jersey, people aren't going to roll over for you. If anything, you have a target on your back, and every week you should expect your opponent's best, because they are gunning to be in your shoes.

That's what my 5–5 sophomore-year team didn't understand, and that's what my junior-year team had to get. We had the talent; we just had to perform on game day, and that's what we started to do. We ended up going on a four-game winning streak, and we even beat our heated rival Holy Spirit at home. We won that game 19–14, and it was one of the most physical games I've ever played in. You could tell by how much effort each person put into every play that this game was serious.

One play sticks out in my mind when I think about that game. We were down 14–13 in the fourth quarter with about three minutes left in the game, and Holy Spirit had the ball on their own twenty-five. It was third and about four, and we needed a stop to get the ball back to try to score and win the game. One of the best football players I ever played with, Josh Moore (LB), came roaring through a seam in the offensive line, and he met Holy Spirit's running back in the backfield. Josh got up, screaming, "Let's go," as he flexed his muscles at the running back on the ground. That play showed me the type of guys we had on this team, specifically Josh. Josh was a very reserved person who didn't say much and was pretty laid back, but when I saw him get up and show that emotion, it was surprising to me. It showed me he really cared. From that point on, I knew I could trust him.

After watching Josh make the play, Phil Paulhill and I locked eyes and were in shock from how enthusiastic Josh was and how amazing the play was. What was so cool about the play Josh made was that he did everything by the book. Because I was at safety that year, I had the perfect view to watch the play develop. Josh stayed square to the line of scrimmage as he flowed in the direction of the ball carrier. However, he wasn't too fast to commit to the ball carrier, which would allow a possible cutback lane to open up. He was patient. Then he took off once the RB made his decision, and from there it was fourth down, and Holy Spirit was punting to us.

As I said, we ended up winning the game, but if Josh Moore hadn't gotten that stop on third down, we probably would have lost that game 14–13. So Josh, thanks, man. We needed you on that play, and you came through.

After that game, Coach Sacco asked me whether I was all right, and I told him I was OK. It was a memorable moment in our relationship. He never was the type to ask whether we were OK after games, but in that game, he could see I had nothing left in me; I had left it all out on the field. It was as if he was gaining more respect for me and he really appreciated my efforts that afternoon.

After the Holy Spirit game, our team was pretty beat up, but we had to recuperate fast because the following Friday night, we had to play an undefeated Saint Augustine Prep. My former high school was rolling that year, and they weren't going to back down because we had some bumps and bruises. We lost 31–16 that night, and I played what was probably my worst game that season. As a team, we couldn't do much either; we just weren't executing at all. It was embarrassing, but I have to give the Prep their props. They were a great team that year.

After the Saint Augustine loss, we bounced back and finished the regular season with two consecutive wins. We were in great shape heading into the playoffs, and we had our sights set on winning a state championship. Now for those who don't understand how the NJSIAA works as far as school groupings, I'm going to explain it for you. In New Jersey, there are numerous state champions in football. We do not have a single state champion at the end of the season, similar to how college football now has the playoff system. Instead, we group schools based on the number of students. Big schools are Group 5, and little schools are Group 1. Everyone else falls into groups in between based on student body size. We also separate schools based on public and nonpublic status. For nonpublic schools, there are Groups 1 through 4. The final way we categorize state champions is by separating the state into north, south, and central divisions. This criterion applies only to public schools; nonpublic schools play schools within their group regardless of where they are in the state. Just so you're clear, this applies only to the playoffs and how they decide who a state champion is. With that being said, our system is flawed, in my opinion, because we never know who the best team in the state is. At the end of the day, we have something like nineteen state champions, and that doesn't make sense to me.

So even though Saint Joseph has won numerous state championships, we technically didn't beat some of the best teams in the state to obtain those accomplishments. I am not saying that we couldn't have beaten those teams, because I'm 100 percent sure that most of those great teams would have dominated the state, regardless of whom we were matched up with. Anyway, let us get back to the story. I know I get sidetracked a lot, but I think it is vital for you to know these things.

I'm not even going to waste your time with the first matchup we had in the playoffs. It was against this team named Pingry, and they were bad. Coach Sacco took the starters out in the third quarter. So let's just get straight to the state-championship game, because that game has a little more worth to it.

I learned many important things in my junior-year state-championship game against Gloucester Catholic, not only about myself but also about my teammates, which was awesome. The game that year was held at Paul IV High School in South Jersey. Before the game, I knew my teammates were ready to go because they had a certain swagger about them. It was a swagger I had been looking for the entire year but could never find. It was as if we had been unsure of ourselves since I got to Saint Joe, but now we were sure. We knew what we were capable of when we played our game. It felt as if I was back playing on my Maullers seventy-pound team with Bill Belton. That type of confidence was back. I felt as prepared as I could be. I was very sure of what I could do on the field, and I finally felt I was in shape enough to get back into the zone. Now we had to go out and put it all out on the field.

Once the game started, I felt comfortable and relaxed. On the first drive, I got an interception from a tipped ball by one of my teammates. I was lucky, but regardless, it was great for the team and our momentum. From watching film all week, we knew we would be able to drive down the field on this team, and that's what we did. I ended up scoring our first TD from thirteen yards out on a 929 sweep. From that point on, I knew we were going to win this game. After my touchdown, my fellow RB Kaheem Reynolds got a score of his own to put us up 14–0. Right before halftime, I scored one more time on a screen pass thrown by our QB Darryl Smith from sixteen yards out.

We were headed into halftime with a 21–0 lead, and we couldn't be stopped. That feeling I had about us being ready was true, and it was great to see our team have all this success early in such a big game. Now we just had to keep it going in the second half. To start the second half, we were getting the ball back first. On the kickoff, Kaheem stole the kick return opportunity by stepping in front of my bro Vinny Reed. It was messed up when I saw it in person, but I couldn't say much, and neither could Vinny, because Kaheem ran that ball back for a ninety-yard TD. We were on fire now, up 28–0. It was getting ugly for Gloucester Catholic.

On the next drive, Gloucester Catholic began to drive down the field on us. A little past midfield, Gloucester Catholic's QB dropped back and threw a slant route in the direction of my bro Phil Paulhill, which was a huge mistake because Phil was starting to dominate out on the edge at corner. When the ball finally got to its destination, it was Phil who made a play on the ball. He had the ball in his hands and then dropped the pick at the last second. He put his hands on his head in disappointment. I walked over to him and gave him an earful. I told him he couldn't be dropping those opportunities in games like this, and my tone wasn't nice when I said it. Instantly, he snapped back and said, "Shut up, G. I know." I could talk to Phil like that because we were close. I knew I would get through to him by being hard on him about that missed opportunity. It sounds like an unusual conversation between friends, but that's just how we communicated, and he knew I wasn't trying to be mean. He just knew he had to make that play.

On the next play, for some reason, Gloucester Catholic's QB tried Phil again, and this time Phil picked the ball off and took it seventy-five yards to the end zone. He was sitting on a five-yard comeback route and timed his break perfectly. I ran all the way down the field to meet him in the end zone to celebrate with him. In the end zone, he joked with me about the conversation we had had the play before. He said, "I wasn't trying to hear your mouth this time, so I knew I had to pick that one off." We continued to laugh about the great play until we saw the flag on the ground. The TD was being called back owing to pass interference on the play. It was a horrible call; Phil never touched the guy. I think the refs were starting to feel bad for our opponents, so they just started to give them calls. All in all, it was a remarkable play by Phil, and an even-better one once we saw it on film the next day.

We ended up winning that game 28–14. We were state champs! However, that moment of glory came and went very fast. I don't know exactly why that was. I think maybe it was because I knew the team we played wasn't that good, which wasn't our fault. If anything, it's the system and the way it's set up in New Jersey. Knowing that there were eighteen other state champs didn't make me feel that proud of my team or myself. Also, we still had one game left, and that was against our crosstown rival, Hammonton High School.

This game against Hammonton was not one I want to remember. We lost that next week, 16–14, on a last-second field goal they shouldn't have had an opportunity to kick in the first place. I'm just going to leave it at that. Just know that we should have won that game and that I slightly separated my right shoulder in the fourth quarter. To the people of Hammonton who may read this book, you got that one, but you also know we helped you win that one. But a win is a win, and I'll leave it at that.

The season was over, and we finished the year 8–3 as state champs. We had lost to Hammonton, Prep, and Bridgeton, so we had a bad year based on Saint Joe expectations, but we had so many positives coming off that season. In that state-championship game, we learned that we had the pieces in place to have a great year next year. I saw that swagger and confidence I knew we had all along. Now we had the entire off-season to get healthy and better as individuals and as a team. My off-season started at physical therapy. I was strengthening that right shoulder I injured in the Hammonton game. But it wasn't that serious an injury, and I recovered fast. Plus, I didn't need surgery.

As the school year was ending, many people from the South Jersey area started to bring in their first couple of scholarship offers from different colleges. I was happy for many of the guys I had met over the years from playing football against them and getting to know them through all-star teams and such. But let's be real; I wanted an offer as well. See, at that point in my life, my dream was to get a scholarship so my parents didn't have to pay for college. Seeing people close to me fulfill that dream made it seem more obtainable. At the same time though, I wasn't getting as much communication from college coaches as other players were. The word "offer" or "scholarship" wasn't even mentioned at any of the meetings I had with college coaches when they came to the school at the end of my junior year. I felt left out, and I was disappointed because I thought I deserved an offer as well. I felt I was just as good as most of the guys getting offers in the area.

I had a conversation with my brother-in-law, Jyi Peterson, who is also my personal trainer, about the scholarship situation and how I felt. I went to Jyi because he himself went through the process and was a highly-recruited player coming out of high school. He was also named an All-American safety during his high school days, so I really respected his opinion on the subject. What Jyi told me that day during our talk honestly changed my life. He said, "Gordon, you're not good enough to deserve an offer yet." I let what he said sink in for a second. Once I grasped what he said, I nodded, telling myself to accept that truth. From there, I asked him what I would have to do to get an opportunity at the next level. He said we were going to have to work, but really work for it. It wasn't going to be easy, or fun, or convenient, but it would be worth it, and that's all I needed to hear.

Jyi, I want to say thank you for keeping it real with me that day. You could have straight up lied to my face, but you didn't. You told me the truth, and I appreciate that. To this day, I have never forgotten what you said. You really did change my life in that moment because you showed me that sometimes we need tough love, and it isn't always going to be nice. Sometimes we don't need nice; we need what's real. From that moment, I allowed myself to be honest with myself about my abilities and how seriously I took my preparation for this game I love. For the next couple of months during training with Jyi, I'd always hear this saying, "It's going to hurt, but it ain't going to kill you," and that kept me going.

THE 856 (SICKLERVILLE)

Throughout my training in the off-season with my brother-in-law, I had these thoughts in the back of my mind. I was thinking about all the people from my area who had come before me. I'm talking about not only Sicklerville (the town I live in) but the entire 856, which is a broad part of South Jersey. In my mind, if I didn't get an offer to go to college, I was letting down not just my family and myself. I was also letting down all the great athletes that had come before me. It sounds a little ridiculous, but that was my mind-set.

I want to lay a little foundation for you so you can understand where I'm going with this. Growing up, I went to multiple high school football games with my parents to see some of the future legends of the 856. However, there were many others dominating the game of football far before I understood what football was. I'm going to name some people that came from the 856 whom I watched either in person, in college, or the pros.

Jeremy Miles (Sicklerville, New Jersey)

I watched Jeremy growing up while he played for the Winslow Eagles in high school. He was tall and lanky but was a great RB and safety. He had elite speed and quickness, which made him stand out from others on the field. Jeremy went on to play at Navy for a couple of years before transferring to UMass and finishing his college career there. He then made his way to the NFL, where he played safety for the Cincinnati Bengals and the Baltimore Ravens.

Julian Talley (Sicklerville, New Jersey)

Julian Talley (or Talley, as people close to him call him) played WR for the Winslow Eagles in high school. I was in middle school when I watched him dominate cornerbacks out on the edge. Talley always had that confidence that you have to have to be a great WR at any level. After high school, Talley attended UMass, where he played alongside New Jersey native Victor Cruz. After college, Talley went on to play WR in the New York Giants organization for a couple of years.

Ka'lial Glaud (Sicklerville, New Jersey)

Ka'lial Glaud (or KG, as everyone calls him) actually was in the Maullers organization when I was playing there as well. KG played high school ball for the Winslow Eagles and played QB and MLB. KG was a beast in high school, but I remember him mostly on the defensive side of the ball just demolishing ball carriers. KG attended Rutgers University, where he continued to master his craft at the linebacker position. After college, KG went on to play for the Tampa Bay Bucs and the Dallas Cowboys.

Shonn Greene (Sicklerville, New Jersey)

I watched Shonn Greene when I was little, and I used to try to do the things he did at the RB position. He used to run over guys and keep moving while he played for the Winslow Eagles in high school. His next step took him to the University of Iowa, where he dominated at the running back position his entire senior year. He played so well that he was awarded the Doak Walker Award, which is given to the nation's best running back in college football. After earning his All-American status in college, Shonn was drafted by the New York Jets, where he played for multiple seasons. He finished his career off with the Tennessee Titans.

Raheem Covington (Pine Hill, New Jersey)

Raheem Covington, who also is my cousin, played cornerback in high school for the Overbrook Rams. I'm not trying to show his age or anything, but I don't remember attending his high school games because I was too young (sorry, cousin). However, Raheem took his talents to Northwestern University, where he was a three-year starter at corner for the Wildcats. I did get to catch one of his games down in Annapolis when he played against Navy, which he played extremely well in. That was the first college game I ever saw in person, and it made me love the game of football even more. After college, Raheem played a couple of years in the CFL.

Ron Dayne (Berlin Township, New Jersey)

For some of you who read this book, Ron Dayne may be a name you recognize right away. For the younger generations, you may not know who he is yet. Growing up, I would always hear stories about Ron Dayne in high school. People in the area to this day call him the best high school running back ever from the area. Like my cousin Raheem Covington, he attended Overbrook High School. Like I said earlier, I was too young to remember any of their high school games, but the stories I heard about him were enough for me. After high school, Ron Dayne went to Wisconsin and destroyed some of college football's oldest records. To this day, he still holds the record for the second-most career rushing yards by a single player (6,397 yards). Not only did he achieve that record, but he also won the Heisman Trophy, which is given to the nation's best player in college football. If you remember, I mentioned Ron Dayne back in chapter 4 when I told you we had the same fifth-grade teacher. Here's a list of awards Ron earned throughout his college career: "Consensus All-American (1999), AP Player of the Year (1999), Maxwell Award (1999), Walter Camp Award (1999), Chic Harley Award (1999), Doak Walker Award (1999), Jim Brown Award (1999), Big Ten Player of the Year (1999), and Rose Bowl MVP (1999, 2000). After college, Ron Dayne was drafted by the New York Giants with the eleventh pick of the

2000 NFL draft. He was with the Giants for five years until moving on to finish his career with the Broncos and the Texans in his last year."

- "Ron Dayne." *Wikipedia*. Wikimedia Foundation, 10 Apr. 2017. Web. 10 Apr. 2017.

Mike Rozier (Camden, New Jersey)

Mike Rozier was a guy who was dominating the game long before I was born. However, that doesn't mean I didn't go back and watch his highlights and do my research on him. When I was in little league, I heard about Mike Rozier for the first time. So I wanted to learn more about him. I learned he attended Woodrow Wilson High School in Camden, New Jersey. He then went to University of Nebraska, where he really made himself a household name throughout the country. I don't want to do Mr. Rozier an injustice by trying to describe how he played. So I recommend if you haven't seen highlights of him, go on Google and YouTube, and see for yourself how great this man was with the ball in his hand. Years before Ron Dayne even knew what the Heisman Trophy was, Mike Rozier already had one of his own after his 1983 college campaign. The pros were the next step for Mr. Rozier. He played a couple of years in the USFL before being drafted by the Houston Oilers in the first round (second overall) of the 1984 NFL Supplemental Draft. He finished his career off with the Atlanta Falcons.

Mike Daniels (Stratford, New Jersey)

I saw him play for the first time in high school. I was going to see my cousin Ahmad Covington (Raheem's little brother) play, and I couldn't help but notice Mike Daniels. They were the two best players on their high school team, Highland Regional. It was cool to see a guy as big as Mike playing running back and just running over, through, and around defenders. After high school I started watching him on TV when he played on Saturdays for the University of Iowa. He played defensive line, and the announcers would always talk about how undersized he was. Regardless of size, Mike Daniels was still constantly interrupting the backfield. Now you can watch Mike play on Sundays for the Green Bay Packers. He's dominant up front, and he not only uses pure strength but also understands leverage and how important a quick first step is.

Chris LaPierre (Medford, New Jersey)

Now, some people may say I'm crazy for this, but in my very biased opinion, I think Chris LaPierre was the best running back in the history of South Jersey. I mean, I already mentioned some guys from our area who have gone on to win Heisman Trophies, and I get that. However, I didn't see those guys with my own eyes. I saw Chris LaPierre live, and when I say he made the game look easy, I mean it. It looked almost as if it was a waste of his time to even go out on the field each game. He'd simply run by people or over them when he played for Shawnee High School. The funniest part of him running the ball was when defenders would seem to get out of his way by "accident." Even though Chris LaPierre was a great football player, he was one of the nation's top lacrosse players, if not the actual best. He was a high school All-American and attended University of Virginia, which in the lacrosse world is like going to Duke for basketball. After a great career at UVA, he went on to play lacrosse professionally. Chris LaPierre was selected number 2 overall in the 2013 Major League Lacrosse Collegiate Draft by the Hamilton Nationals, but he began his rookie season with the Florida Launch in 2014. He now plays for the New York Lizards.

Logan Ryan (Berlin, New Jersey)

Logan Ryan was a cornerback who played for Eastern High School. I used to watch him get matched up against Julian Talley when he played against Winslow. In my eyes, Logan was a technician when it came to the position. His next step was going to Rutgers University, where he played alongside many 856 guys, including Ka'lial Glaud. At Rutgers, Logan solidified himself as one of the most consistent corners in the nation. His playing style gave Bill Belichick enough confidence to draft him in the third round of the NFL draft. Since then, Logan has been a vital part of the New England Patriots defensive backfield. He also is a Super Bowl champion, which is pretty awesome. He currently plays for the Tennessee Titans.

Joe Flacco (Audubon, New Jersey)

A lot of you are probably familiar with the name Joe Flacco. I mentioned him in chapter 2 when I played in a little league championship game at his high school. Joe Flacco was the man in South Jersey when he played at Audubon High School. Every weekend he'd be in the *Courier Post*, and I'd see a picture of him with an article right next to it. After high school, Joe Flacco went to Pittsburgh to continue his career and education. However, that didn't work out for him, and he ended up transferring to the University of Delaware. At Delaware, Joe Flacco was still the man. My dad would always keep me updated on how he was doing because he was a local guy; plus my dad was a University of Delaware alum. He was proud of his team and how successful they were. I don't have to tell you what happened after that. But for the people who don't know, Joe Flacco went on to be the starting QB of the Baltimore Ravens. He even won Super Bowl XLVII and won the game's MVP Award.

You know how they say we all are products of our environments? Well, this is whom I knew about growing up. I was following, watching, and researching all these people. As I got into high school, I felt I needed to add to this great list of athletes from the 856. It was a pride thing for me. It was as if I didn't want to let them down. I'm so proud of where I'm from; I just wanted to make a name for myself so those who came before me would be proud of me as well. It was as if I had an obligation to be a successful athlete, because that's all the 856 puts out. I mean, really, what other area code can say they have two Heisman Trophy winners? I didn't do the research, but I highly doubt it's happened again. But regardless, you get my point. And I didn't even mention all the great football players from the 856. I left numerous people out, and to those people, I'm sorry. I just wanted to give people who aren't from the 856 an understanding of how significant it is, in my opinion, to be from the 856.

Two people I want to mention who are from the 856 but aren't football players are Mike Trout and Jordan Burroughs.

Mike Trout (Millville, New Jersey)

Going to see Mike Trout play baseball in high school was a must if you lived in the area. The first time I saw him play, I thought to myself, "Wow, this guy is good." This is obviously before I knew who he was or who he was going to be. But watching him for that first time in high school showed me that my game had a lot of maturing to do. We played two different sports, but there was something about his game. It was proven and established. He had a professional swagger, if that makes sense. When I was a kid from the area trying to fulfill my own dreams, he showed me how much growing I needed to do to get where I wanted to be. Mike, I just want to say thank you for doing what you do. Also, thanks for always representing South Jersey and the 856 very well. I appreciate that.

Jordan Burroughs (Sicklerville, New Jersey)

Jordan Burroughs is also a Sicklerville native and is, in my opinion, the best athlete in the country regardless of sport. I've known him since my little league wrestling days. He was one of the older guys in the wrestling room. As he got older, he stuck with wrestling, and during his senior year of high school, he was a state champion. He took his talents to Nebraska to continue his education and love for the sport. At Nebraska, Jordan started to thrive and become the athlete he is today. Once Jordan went pro, he didn't stop winning. He lives up to his twitter name (@alliseeisgold) because in 2012 in London, Jordan won an Olympic Gold medal for the United States. Jordan also is a four-time world champion and winner of twenty- two international championships. If you asked Jordan what his biggest accomplishment is, he'd most likely tell you having the privilege of being the father of his two beautiful children.

Jordan, I want to say thank you for being an inspiration to me as you continue your success. One thing you did for kids from our hometown was show them how obtainable their dreams can be. You made it realistic. You walked down the same hallways as they did and went food shopping with your parents at the same places. You weren't a farfetched sports figure; you were just Jordan Burroughs from Sicklerville. Keep doing what you're doing. I'm proud of you. In my eyes, you're the Michael Jordan of wrestling.

All these people are an inspiration to me every day. They make me put my best foot forward and make me proud of where I'm from. I want to say thank you to every single one of you for the impact you have had on my life.

Now or Never

With the 856 greats in the back of my mind, my legacy on the line, and a scholarship offer nowhere to be found; motivation came at a surplus. That entire summer before camp, almost every single night, Jyi and I would work out somewhere in Winslow. Any given night, you could find us working out on Winslow High School's track and football field or lifting at the gym Shapes to Come. It was like clockwork. After a while, the nights blended together, and it was all just a blur. And when I say "nights," I mean it; Jyi would not be back in our area after work until about six. Every night, he would come straight from work to the track, where I'd already be warming up. When we first started training that summer, I fought Jyi constantly about changing the time of training. I was about to be a senior in high school, and it was the summertime. I wanted to hang out with my friends and chill. Jyi would remind me that sometimes when you have a goal you want to achieve, the process of achieving that goal might not be convenient. However, it's necessary if it's important enough to you.

He was right. I really wanted to get an offer, and this is what it took. Some nights the workouts were long and grueling and felt as if they'd never end. I never said anything, but some nights I was so frustrated with Jyi. I'd get mad because the workout would kill my legs to the point where I almost couldn't walk. We ran so much you would have thought I was training to be on Team USA's track team. But I knew it would all be worth it in the end, so I kept working.

On Saturdays, we ran hills at Donio Park. I have to tell you about the greatness of Donio Park before I move on. Donio Park is a huge circular park in the middle of Sicklerville. Just imagine a meteor from space coming down and hitting Earth. Now imagine the hole in the ground. That's Donio Park. The purpose it serves is really a blessing. It's not only the home of the Winslow Maullers, the little league football team I played for. It is also a runner's paradise. A path runs along the top of the perimeter of the entire park, which people run every day. Many athletes use the hills that surround the entire park. Since I was a little kid, I have been running hills at Donio. My theory is that we have great athletes in this area because we've all run those hills our entire lives. Also, because there are so many fields available anytime, the park is perfect to get a seven-on-seven going or one-on-ones. OK, so that's Donio Park in a nutshell.

Jyi, I want to say thanks for taking the time to train me. I took time away from your wife and kids, but you stuck with me, and I appreciate that.

Moving forward a little brings us to summer practice of my senior year. This was a great time because I felt unstoppable out on the field. I felt great at practice. All the hard work I had put in during the summer with Jyi paid off, and I could feel it. I could run for days and never get tired, which I loved. I was looking forward to the first time I could showcase all this hard work in a real game setting, or at least a scrimmage.

Our first scrimmage that year was against Mainland, and I couldn't wait for it. It was time to give my teammates and coaches a preview of what they could expect from me. Plus, in the back of my mind at all times was the reminder that I didn't have a scholarship offer. Going into that scrimmage—really, the entire year—I had a chip on my shoulder.

When the scrimmage started, we defensively dominated Mainland and kept their playmakers contained. When we finally got the ball on offense, my eyes lit up because I knew what I was about to do to these guys. It was just a matter of Coach Sacco calling my number. After calling a couple of run plays for my teammates Kaheem and Eli, Coach Sacco finally gave me the ball. The call was speed toss to the wide side of the field, one of my favorite plays to run. We got set, the ball was hiked, and Darryl tossed me the ball. It was time to create. I have to give my offensive line and the running backs who blocked for me a lot of credit because they did a tremendous job of blocking on this play. I didn't even see a would-be tackler until I got into the secondary. As I turned the corner and got vertically up the field, I saw the safety breaking down in preparation to tackle me. As I was running toward him with a full head of steam, I thought to myself that this kid was undersized to be playing safety. After surveying the situation, I decided to run right over him since he was much smaller than I was. And that's exactly what I did. I lowered my shoulder at about the fifteen-yard line going in and ran this kid over so hard that he bounced off me. The back of his helmet hit the ground, and I stepped right over him and continued to run into the end zone for our first touchdown of the day. One of my teammates and good friends, Kaiwan Lewis, was the first one to meet me in the end zone to celebrate. He said to me, "Why did you run that kid over like that, G?" The only response I had for him was that I needed an offer and that's why I did it.

I ran over to the sideline, and Coach Sacco said, "Great run, G." I told Coach I wasn't playing offense anymore, because those kids were a waste of my time and energy. He didn't say anything; he just smiled and looked away. That was a big moment in our relationship. He understood what I was going to bring to the table that year and that he could trust me. We ended up beating Mainland in that scrimmage, and it was a great way to get our team warmed up for the season.

To open up the season, we started hot. In our season opener, we beat Buena 40–0, and in week 2 we handled Middle Township pretty well with a score of 55–0. Those were good wins, but they didn't mean much to us. I mean, they helped us figure things out as a team, but we knew the real competition was soon to come. It didn't take long: good ol' Holy Spirit was on the schedule for week 3. We knew they were gunning for us since we had beaten them at home the previous year. This year they had a stacked team, and there was talent at every position. They had some guys on their team that could ball, like Joe Callahan, Tim Goodwin, Donta Pollack, Ethan Gambale, and Zach Fabel, to name just a few.

I can't forget to mention the toughest player I ever played against in high school: Joe Sarnese. The guy was just a football player, and he did everything well. Offensively he was a threat at WR, and defensively he was probably the best defender in South Jersey, if not the entire state, via the safety position. He also was incredibly dependable and had big-play ability as a returner. So if we wanted to win, we would have to stop him from being a huge factor.

Prior to the game, the media blew this game out of proportion, as they always do. Media from all over attended this game. It felt as if every day during that week of practice, someone would come to get a quote from one of my teammates about the game. Coach Sacco told us not to say too much to the media and just focus on the task at hand. He was never one for talking about an opponent before a game, and neither was I.

When Friday night rolled around, it was game time down in Absecon, New Jersey, where Holy Spirit was located. In the locker room, you could tell we had a quiet confidence about ourselves, but at the same time, we had a lot of respect for our opponent. They were good, and we weren't going to ignore that. My friend Todd asked me his usual pregame question: "Are you nervous?" My sophomore year I had lied and told him no, I wasn't. This year, however, I was 100 percent certain I wasn't nervous. Somewhere around my junior year, I stopped getting that nervous feeling. I always felt so prepared, both physically and mentally, and when you're prepared for something, why be nervous?

After the pregame speech by our coaches, we headed down to the field. I was so locked in during pregame warm-ups. While we were doing our DB drills, I noticed all the scouts from big schools in attendance. Schools like Notre Dame, Tulsa, Tulane, North Carolina, South Carolina, Rutgers, and Boston College were all there. No pressure, but I knew my teammates and I had to play well. I had played in big games before, but this one was the biggest stage in my life thus far.

Holy Spirit won the toss and chose to receive the ball first. Right away they tried to go deep on us. The first play of the game, Joe Callahan dropped back and fired a bomb to Joe Sarnese, but he forgot about one thing: my boy Phil Paulhill, the best corner in the state that year. As he was that entire year, Phil was in perfect position to make a play on the ball, and that's exactly what he did. Phil caught an interception that threw all the momentum in our direction. Everyone on our sideline went crazy, and Phil was amped up after making the big play. Now on offense, we drove right down the field on Holy Spirit. That first offensive possession, Coach kept feeding me the ball. Three yards and a cloud of dust were all we needed to get to the end zone, and it seemed that was all we could get against that tough Holy Spirit defense. It seemed every time I had a chance to break loose for a big gain, I was one-on-one with Joe Sarnese. I have to give him credit. Every single time we were one-on-one in a little bit of space, he made the for-sure tackle on me. He understood angles and could decipher how plays would develop in an instant. It almost felt as if he was meeting me damn near at the line of scrimmage every time I got the ball, yet he played ten to twelve yards from the line of scrimmage.

Eventually, we got down to the five-yard line, and it was fourth down. Coach Sacco called a pass play that went to Pat Casey, our tight end. The ball was snapped, Darryl dropped back, and he had Pat wide open in the back of the end zone, but Darryl overthrew him, and we lost that opportunity. I mean, it was an easy throw to make, to be honest, but we're all human, and we mess up sometimes. I could tell my coaches and some of my teammates couldn't believe what they had just seen. I wasn't worried though. The game had just started, and I was sure we would get another opportunity to punch it in.

Now back on defense, we allowed Holy Spirit to push the ball out of their end zone. With the ball placed in the middle of the field, we were expecting another shot downfield from Callahan to Sarnese. At least that's what the scouting report said to expect, and sure enough, that's what we got. On second down, somewhere around midfield, Joe Callahan dropped back and threw another bomb to Joe Sarnese. I don't know why they kept trying my brother Phil Paulhill, but they did, and it bit them in the butt again. It was another interception for Phil. I was so happy for him; he was having the game of his life on such a big stage.

Back on offense, we had to get something started. After a couple of runs, Coach Sacco called a waggle, which is a pass play we were famous for. On this particular play, I managed to leak out of the backfield uncovered, and Darryl found me in the flat wide open. I caught the ball and tried to make my way upfield, but I slipped and fell. See, I forgot to mention that there was a big controversy about the condition of Holy Spirit's field that night. It was really muddy and not kept up very well, so great footing was hard to come by. But that's not an excuse, because both teams had to play on it.

When I fell to the ground, I was so upset, and I could hear a big roar of frustration from our sideline because they knew if I hadn't fallen, it would most likely have been a touchdown. What I saw when I had turned my head upfield before falling was nothing but green grass, and I realized I had missed that opportunity. After that, we had to punt and give the ball back to Holy Spirit with decent field position.

I'm going to get straight to it: the rest of the game was an embarrassment for our program. We ended up losing 35–0, but the score didn't reflect how good they were or how badly we played that day. For some reason, our center Delonce Hargraves and quarterback Darryl Smith just kept fumbling the exchange. We lost the ball four times owing to a bad exchange of the snap. It made us look as if we were an unorganized team that didn't have any business being on the same field as those guys. Coach Sacco ended up pulling Darryl from the starting quarterback position and replacing him with the young guy, Anthony Giagunto. We finished the game fighting, but we walked off that field feeling defeated. I felt bad for Darryl because everyone was getting on him and blaming him for our loss.

Darryl, I just want to say I was a little frustrated when Delonce and you were fumbling the snap, but that was just because I'm competitive and wanted to win. I was never mad directly at you or Delonce. I want you to know I don't think you or Delonce were the reason we lost. I mean, if the defense had played better and never let them score thirty-five points, none of the things that went down after that game probably would have ever happened. I want you to understand that when you were benched, it was a weird situation for a couple of the guys on the team who were close with you. You are a friend, and to see you in the place you were in was weird, because I felt we kept moving forward as a team and we were leaving you behind or by the wayside. That gave me an uneasy feeling, but at the same time, whether you want to say it or not, Ant came in and did a great job as well. If that Holy Spirit game had never happened, I'm positive you would have had the same success he did, if not more, because you were both great players. All in all, I want you to know that that loss wasn't all your fault.

After that loss, we weren't in shock, but we knew we were better than what the final score showed. For the rest of the season, we had a unique type of focus about us. The week after the Holy Spirit game, the coaches were hard on us, but it wasn't for long, because we were a mature group. We knew what we had done wrong and could correct our mistakes. For the next few weeks, we dominated our opponents and let up only one touchdown. Everything was going well, until the team got the news that Coach Sacco was sick and would be in the hospital for a while.

When we first heard what happened to Coach, everybody was shaken up. Coach was the type of person who never wanted to show weakness, so to hear this was surprising. I had seen him squatting 375 pounds and benching 415 pounds twenty-four hours prior to the news, so hearing this threw me off. They said he had a brain aneurysm. I didn't know what that was, but it sounded bad, and it *was* bad if it took Coach away from the field. All we could do was wait and pray for Coach's recovery.

Coach Mueriello was our interim head coach as we headed into the semifinals of the playoffs. We were matched up with an undefeated Saint Anthony team that was 10–0, and they were definitely on their high horse. Before Coach Sacco got sick, he told me that their coach tried to make fun of our team during one of their conversations a couple of days prior to the game. Their coach said he never heard of our team, yet we had the record for most state championships won and most state-championship appearances, and we were top three in the state for playoff appearances. If anything, we didn't know much about their football program. When people talk about Saint Anthony's in New Jersey, you hear about how good they are in basketball but never football.

Regardless, the Saint Anthony's coach was tripping for taking a shot at our program. But don't worry; he learned quickly that he had made a mistake. With Coach Sacco being sick and in the hospital during the game, we had some extra motivation. On November 19, 2010, we headed up to Jersey City to give the Friars of Saint Anthony the proper ass whooping (excuse my language) they deserved. With Coach Rick and Coach Stalba collaborating on the play calls, they brought everything out of the bag. You have to understand that Coach Sacco was old school and stuck in his ways with play selection. He liked the good old fundamental Wing-T play calls. With the younger generation now at the helm, we ran every play in the book, and we ran them to perfection. We ended up putting forty points up on that Saint Anthony's team.

But offense wasn't the only thing firing on all cylinders. Our defense that game was relentless. I don't know whether it was because we were playing harder for Coach or we just wanted to make it to the state-championship game. Regardless, we were like animals when it came to defense. That game, people were so hungry to make a tackle that we started betting money on who would make the next play. We ended up shutting that team out for four quarters and left the field with a 40–0 victory. (This is a little sidenote, but I was so confident during that game that someone took a picture of me at halftime listening to music, and I ended up posting it on Facebook during halftime. And to those thinking it, no, I never did that again at any level, because it's childish and unnecessary and will get you a fine in the NFL.)

The day after the Saint Anthony game, the whole team was in a great mood because we knew we had played to our full potential. However, the best news was that Coach Sacco was out of the hospital and was coming to watch film after missing a couple of days. When he finally got back to the field house, we were happy to see him, but we could tell he was weak. He moved a little slow, and we could see he had lost a bunch of weight in just days. He also talked very quietly, and when he did talk, he was brief. That day we watched film with Coach, and it was like that moment when you receive an A+ on a big test and your parents are extremely proud of you. Coach watched quietly and looked pleased with the way we had performed both individually and as a group. He didn't say much, but when he was done watching the film, he showed some signs of the old him by giving us a little smirk and letting us know we played well.

After Coach had the surgery, he wasn't the same at all. He was still himself, but I think he learned a lot from what happened to him. He had a new appreciation for and outlook on life. Football was important to Coach, but I think after his incident, he realized that it was just a game and that there are more important things in this world, like family. Even though he was the same, this changed him a little, and it affected our whole team and how we communicated with him. There wasn't that much joking around during practice, because Coach didn't have time for that. He had to sit down and rest for a couple of minutes if he stood too long during practice. The man had almost died a couple of days ago and it seriously changed the vibe around our program, but it was positive.

With Coach getting better day by day, we were headed into Hammonton week. This was an extremely important game for us because it was against our crosstown rival. In addition, Coach Sacco was from Hammonton, so we wanted to make sure he, along with the school, had bragging rights in town for at least another year. Plus, they had beaten us the year prior at home, so we had to get some revenge.

This year, the game was played at Hammonton's field. For some reason I loved playing on their field. I don't know what it was about that field, but I felt comfortable and relaxed there. This was a big game for Coach Sacco because it was his first game back since his time in the hospital. Many people questioned whether he should even coach this game in the first place; Coach Rick had done such a great job the last week, and people were concerned for Coach's health. But regardless of what others thought, Coach was on the sideline that game, doing what he did best.

The game started slow for us as we let up an early touchdown, but we weren't flustered, because we knew the mistakes we had made. A couple of drives later, my big little bro Max Valles recovered a fumble and ran it back to the end zone to tie the game up 7–7. For the rest of the first half, there was a lot of back-and-forth, and neither team could get the ball moving. Heading into halftime, we were tied up 7–7 with Hammonton. I wasn't pleased with our performance as a team because I knew we should have been winning.

Running into the locker room for halftime, I realized I had touched the ball only three times the entire half. If you know me or have ever played football with me, you know I was never the kid who complained or even made a comment about getting the ball. However, in this situation, I felt that by getting the ball a little more, I could help my team win this game. So I went up to my running backs coach, Coach Stalba, and told him that I had gotten the ball only three times in the first half. I said, "Now, Coach, I don't know if Coach Sacco literally forgot to give me the ball this half because of his brain surgery, but I can't help this team if you guys don't allow me to do what I do. So help me help you."

After I shared my thoughts with my running backs coach, he quickly shared the information with the rest of the coaching staff while they met outside the locker room, as they usually did. After I sat in the locker room with my teammates for about three minutes, the coaches came storming in with the game plan for the second half. Coach Sacco said, "Offensive line, get ready, because we're giving the ball to Gordon twenty-plus times, and we're going to run it down their throats."

That was it. That was all he said; then they walked out. It may not have shown on the surface, but I was super excited and, more importantly, ready physically and mentally. I finished the game with two touchdowns and 125+ yards. More importantly, we won the game 20–8. I really want to take the time to thank my offensive line and the other running backs for blocking for me that day. I understand that you can be the most talented person in the world, but if you don't have great blocking, it doesn't matter. Thank you, guys, for doing a great job all year long. You deserve most of the credit for my success. So once again, thank you. I literally couldn't have done it without you. I also want to thank Coach Sacco and Coach

Stalba for believing in me and putting the ball in my hands that day against Hammonton. I appreciate the trust you had in me, and thank you for allowing me to help our team.

With the Hammonton game behind us, the team's focus and mine were on the state-championship game. We were excited because it was the first time our team had ever played at Rutgers Stadium. When we first pulled up to the stadium, I thought, "Wow, I would love to play in a stadium like this for the next four years." Being there really drove home the fact that I didn't have an offer yet. But that wasn't my focus for the night; I was trying to win my last high school game and go out as a champion.

When I got into the locker room, I noticed an envelope with my name on it next to all my stuff. It was a letter from my mom. When I started reading it, I started to cry instantly. I wasn't bawling my eyes out, but let's just say it was hard to hold back the tears and emotion. The letter was a commemoration of the times we had shared the past four years in high school and the experiences we had gone through as a mother and a son. It covered all the hardships and the good times we had together. Plus, my mom went into the times when I was a little baby and I had brain surgery and she thought I was going to die. That part really got me. All in all, it was touching, and it made me appreciate not only my mother for everything she'd done for me but also where I was in life at that moment. Thanks, Mom.

After wiping away the tears and getting my focus in line, it was now time to ball with my squad one last time. If I wasn't already emotional from the letter, knowing this was my last time playing with this group of guys just added to this magnificent, memorable moment.

While walking down the tunnel at Rutgers Stadium, I thought about many things: my future, my family, my friends, the past seventeen years of my life, and whether I had done enough to leave a mark at Saint Joseph High School as one of the best players ever to wear this jersey. I didn't know the answer then, but I was going to use this last opportunity to finish this chapter of my young life. I know some of you want me to go in depth with the football aspect of this book, but as I said earlier, this book isn't only about football. It's more about the relationships it helped create. So

I'm just going to tell you we won the game that night 40–0. We dominated as a team in every aspect. A couple of my close friends played great games, and I didn't have a bad game either. Rushing, I actually had the best game of my high school career, in my opinion, with 208 yards and three touchdowns on the day. I felt invincible out there that day. I was in the zone again. But I don't ever want to forget that offensive line. I said it before, but you guys know you made my job easy and allowed me to be successful. So once again, thank you.

After the game, I was in such a great mood. I don't know what euphoria feels like, but that was the closest I've ever been to it. On the bus back home, my teammates and I were talking about life and how we had done it again. We had finished on top as state champs. I'd be lying if I told you I wasn't already thinking about college on that bus ride back home, because I was. I didn't know what the future held for me, but I was nervous and excited about it at the same time.

The next couple of weeks following the state-championship game victory was a weird time for me. I started to receive many accolades from all these different newspapers from the area. I even finished as the third-highest scorer in South Jersey that year, with 136 points. All that sounds nice, but I still didn't have any scholarship offers from any schools. Things just didn't add up. I wasn't a bad kid, and I never got in trouble. My GPA after four years of high school was 3.75, and my SAT (two-part) score was over 1000, so it couldn't have been my grades. I didn't get it. Did schools just not think I was good enough? Trust me: I asked myself every question in the book.

Even though I didn't mention it earlier, I had been getting a little buzz from colleges as early as my sophomore year. But it was never serious, in my opinion. I went on some unofficial visits, but nothing major. During the last three weeks of my senior season, a whole bunch of college coaches came to school to talk and exchange film. But there still was no offer on the table when my senior season was over. I hate to compare my situation to others', but when people in my area were already committed to colleges, I was at home waiting for the phone to ring. For about three weeks after the championship game, I questioned myself. Was I good enough to play college football at the Division 1 level? Would I let myself down and let my dream of getting a scholarship fade away? I even thought about whether I should keep playing football. See, I'm my biggest critic, so I'm always the hardest on myself.

One day, while I was in the weight room with my friends Pat Casey and Phil Paulhill, we were talking about college. We all thought we should have had an offer from at least one school by now. I mean, we had finished the season as state champs (10–1), and all three of us had contributed to our team's success tremendously. We were frustrated, and we went to talk to Coach about how we felt. We shared our thoughts with Coach Sacco, and we asked him to make a push for us to help us get scholarship opportunities. All Coach Sacco said was, "I'm not going to sugarcoat anything to these coaches," and then he walked away.

I was even more frustrated after hearing that; I didn't understand what that meant. He didn't have to sugarcoat anything for me. I simply wanted him to let these college coaches know I was ready for the next level and I would be an awesome player for any team. There was nothing to sugarcoat. I'm not trying to sound cocky, but I thought, "I just helped this man win another state championship." In both my junior- and senior-year state-championship games, I was the player of the game. So what was there to sugarcoat? All my numbers were there, and the film spoke for itself. So why wasn't I getting any love from colleges? I just didn't get it. I was mad at the world for a brief time, but I realized that wouldn't change anything. So I used that frustration at the gym every day after school, still patiently waiting for a call from some university.

An Early Christmas Present
(The Recruiting Process)

At this point in my senior year, it was winter break, and I was focused on where I was going to college. My mother was a teacher for twenty-seven years (newly retired), and all she wanted me to do was go to college. Every day after the last game of the season, she asked me about applying to college. All year long, I told her not to worry about the college-application process, but she didn't want to hear that. She wanted to make sure her baby was going to school. To be real, that entire season I avoided filling out an application. Not only did it take too long, but I also figured I'd get a scholarship—except that plan wasn't working, as you know, so Mom was getting worried. I was in the gym every day training, waiting for a call. I figured I was going to get a call from Stony Brook first because I had dominated their one-day camp and their coach came to see me three times during the season. Unfortunately, I still didn't have an offer from them. Other teams that seemed to be interested were Sacred Heart University and the University at Albany, along with a few others.

The entire recruiting process for the last four years had been extremely draining for me. I'd be in class just thinking about the opportunity to get a scholarship and help my parents out financially. It never left my mind. It was as if every decision I made in high school was made to get me to that goal. The fact that I still hadn't achieved that goal, and it was already December of my senior year, bothered me. As I said before, I questioned my abilities and contemplated whether I would even play in college. But I knew I was good enough. I just didn't understand why I wasn't getting a chance.

This process was difficult not only for me but also for my parents. I'm not a parent, but I can see how my child not fulfilling his or her goals could affect me as well. All parents want to see their kids be successful and achieve their goals, and I can only imagine how tough it is on you when they don't. Especially when you know they put the work and time in to put themselves in the position to get an opportunity like the one I had within arm's reach.

You can call me soft all you want, but I'm not going to lie to you: there were many nights in my room when I would just cry. But I'll tell you this: those tears showed me how much I loved the game and how much I wasn't ready to let it go. I just didn't get it. I knew I was good enough and had done everything right. I was in a funk for a minute; I was down on myself and constantly had negative thoughts come in and out of my head about the entire process.

The day was either December 21 or 22 of 2010 (I forget which day it was, but it was one of those days). I was driving back home from the weight room, as I had done every day since the state game, and my phone rang. It was Coach Ryan McCarthy from the University at Albany. My eyes lit up when I saw who was calling. I answered the phone, and as coaches usually do, he started the conversation with a little small talk. You know, the usual, asking about the family and how school was going. Truthfully, I was trying to get down to business. I wanted to know one thing: was he going to offer me or not? I wasn't trying to be disrespectful. That was just my mind-set at the time. A couple of minutes into the conversation, Coach McCarthy finally said, "Gordon, we really like you as a player on film, and we would like to verbally offer you. We also want to set up a visit for you in the near future." I was so happy I didn't even know what to say. I probably was mumbling my words, and I forget what I said next. I just remember being really happy. After the conversation was over, I said thank you to Coach McCarthy and then hung up. At that moment I started dancing uncontrollably in my car. It was probably hilarious if anyone saw me, but I didn't care; I was ecstatic.

Right after getting off the phone with Coach McCarthy from Albany, I called Coach Kevin Bolis from Sacred Heart University. Before I continue, let me tell you how I got in touch with Sacred Heart University (SHU). Most players meet coaches when they come to their high schools on their usual visits. That's how I met Coach McCarthy, and from there we exchanged film. My process with SHU and Coach Bolis was a little different. See, my cousin Ahmad Covington was the starting cornerback for SHU at the time, and I had contacted him right after my senior season was over. I talked to him and asked him to share my film with his coaches since I didn't have any offers. From there, Coach Bolis e-mailed me and said that he liked what he saw on film and was going to come by the school to visit my teammates and I.

You should also know that when Coach Bolis met with me in person for the first time, he was super awkward. Well, that's what I thought at first. He came in the office, shook my hand very firmly, and showed no emotion on his face. Most coaches come in and are excited or at least intrigued when they meet a player they have an interest in, but he was different. He acted almost as if he was disinterested in being there. He didn't sell the school or the football program to us, as everyone else did. He just said, "My name is Coach Bolis. I coach at Sacred Heart University, a small 1AA school in Connecticut that plays in the Northeast Conference (NEC). We aren't very good at the moment, but we're working on getting better, and our academics are solid. That's all I've got. Do you have any questions?" That's what he said, or at least that's what I heard. But what Coach Bolis did was amazing, because he found a way to stand out from the pack. See, every other coach that came to our school tried to sell his school as if it was the greatest place in the world even if it wasn't, and that started to get repetitive after a while. I knew they were going to say the same things every time. His approach was different, and it made me want to learn more about SHU. I guess he had the concept of reverse psychology down to a T, because it worked on me.

That's the quick story on Coach Bolis and our first-time meeting each other in person. So thank you Ahmad. I appreciate it cousin. It all started with you.

To continue what I was saying earlier, I called Coach Bolis right after talking to Coach McCarthy. See, what I learned in this process is that the players have the power in their hands once they get an offer. For some reason, coaches are more likely to offer you a scholarship if you already have one, especially if you have an offer from someone in their conference. In my situation, I had received one verbally from Albany seconds before. With this leverage, I confidently got Coach Bolis on the phone. Once again, our conversation started with a little small talk. Then I got straight to the point, and it went a little something like this: "So Coach, I just got my first offer from Albany today, but I'm still really interested in Sacred Heart. Is there any way we can make this work for both of us?" Coach Bolis seemed fascinated and proceeded to tell me that he would give me a call the next day for sure. He was on the road recruiting, and tomorrow he would be back at school.

So when tomorrow came, I got that call from Coach Bolis as he had promised. Like clockwork, he verbally offered me right there on the spot. I was so happy because now I had not one offer but two. My next thought turned to whom I could contact from bigger schools at the 1AA and 1A level. But then I realized that all those bigger schools already had their recruiting classes finalized and their main recruits verbally committed. I wasn't content, but I was thankful for the opportunity these two programs and universities gave me. The way I looked at it, if these bigger schools had wanted me, they would have been in contact with me months ago. By this point we were only sixty days away from signing day.

The next step for me was setting up my official visits to both Albany and SHU. I had my Albany visit set up for January 11–12 and my SHU visit for January 13–14. So it was busy week for my parents and I, but it was important. Heading up to Albany first was fun. For one, I had never been to that part of New York before. I was also excited to go there because they were the first ones to offer me. I have always had, and still do have, great respect for the entire coaching staff and university for believing in me when no one else did. When we finally got to campus, I was feeling myself (I felt like the man, for those who don't know what that means). We did the usual campus tour and Q&A with the players and then dinner with the coaches and their wives. But the part I loved the most was when they brought us to Jillian's, which was a Dave & Buster's type of place. Just imagine a big arcade for adults that also serves food and has pool tables and a sports bar type of feel. After that, we went to a couple parties with our host that night.

The next morning, I got up super early and met with the legendary Coach Ford and received my actual scholarship agreement. Now let me tell you what really went down in that room. Albany offered me $5,000 a year with the possibility to earn more once I became a starter. They also told me I would have to redshirt right away. I was torn with emotions; one side of me was thankful, and the other was ready to snap. I truly appreciated them giving me the money and the opportunity to earn more, but $5,000? I mean, Albany didn't cost that much to start with, so that did help, but I would still have to pay about $15,000 a year. I was calm and collected, but I could tell my mom was mad. She was looking at Coach Ford like, "Five thousand dollars?" I could tell she was about to snap, so I wanted to get her out of there as soon as possible. After the offer was given and we said our good-byes, we got in the car and headed to SHU.

Instantly, Mom started going off. She felt they were disrespecting me, because my talent and abilities were worth more than $5,000 a year. I agreed with her, but I tried to keep it cool and be thankful. Plus, Coach McCarthy had told me if more money was freed up, then it was definitely going to me. So I was hopeful and optimistic about that.

After a couple of hours in the car driving from Albany, New York, to Fairfield, Connecticut, it felt great to finally stretch my legs. When we got to SHU, I was tired since I had gotten only three hours of sleep the night before. We were a little late to the festivities already going on with the recruits who had arrived earlier. But it wasn't a problem, because the coaches knew I was coming straight from Albany. Trust me: I didn't keep that a secret. When we first arrived, my parents and I got a personal tour of the facilities and campus since we had missed the one earlier during the designated time. My first impression of SHU's campus was that it was beautiful even though there was still a lot of construction going on. The thing that stood out to me right away was how clean it was; those who know me well know I'm a clean freak. After the tours of the athletic center and campus, we finally met up with the rest of the recruits on campus that week.

The first coach I met that day was Coach Darin Edwards. He was the defensive line coach and the token black coach on the staff (that is a joke, but seriously though, he was). Coach Edwards had some swag to him and was very personable. After saying hi, the next thing Coach Edwards said to me was, "So how much money did Albany give you?" I hadn't expected him to ask me that right away and was kind of thrown off. With a little hesitation, I told him the truth: $5,000. He laughed and said, "That's it?" He told me they didn't really want me if that's all they were offering me as we walked into the huge room where the other recruits were conversing. After that, my parents started to talk to Coach Edwards while I went over and talked to Coach Bolis and introduced myself to all the other coaches I didn't know.

A couple of minutes later, my cousin Ahmad, whom I mentioned earlier, came into the room, and we started catching up since I hadn't seen him in a while. He introduced me to his good friend Reuben McIntosh, who also played DB there at SHU. After a couple of minutes in the meeting room with the coaches, parents, and other recruits, Ahmad, Reub, and I all went back to their room.

We played video games for a little bit while we talked about life and football. Then as it got late, they asked me whether I wanted to go out. I kept it real with them and told them I was fatigued from the night before, so all I wanted to do was grab some food and go to sleep. So that's what we did. It actually was a great night. We went to this place called Coyote Jack's, which was amazing. I don't know whether I was just really hungry or what, but that food hit the spot. They must've had the best chicken quesadillas in the world, because I'll tell you what: I remember that day as if it was yesterday simply because of that food. But don't let me get sidetracked.

After we ate, we headed back to Ahmad and Reub's dorm and just chilled. I got my blanket and crashed on the couch at about ten o'clock. I woke up the next morning and felt so refreshed. I really needed that sleep. Once I got myself together, I headed to the athletic center, a.k.a. the Pitt Center, and met back up with the coaches and my parents. After about fifteen minutes, while eating breakfast, my parents and I were called up to meet with the head coach, Paul Gorham.

It felt like déjà vu since I had done the same thing twenty-four hours before at Albany. We talked to Coach Gorham, and he gave me the offer. They were offering me $10,000 in academic money and $15,000 athletic. Now that sounds like a lot more than what Albany offered, but Albany was also a lot cheaper. Sacred Heart cost about $45,000 while Albany cost only $20,000. So technically, Albany was cheaper to attend. Once again, I appreciated what they offered me and heard out what the man had to say. Just like at Albany, I could tell my mom was upset, but this time she didn't show it as much.

Just a side note to all parents and recruits, please understand that just because you get an offer from a school does not mean it's always a full scholarship. I want to clear that up.

After all the good-byes and handshakes, we got back in the car and headed back to Sicklerville. The three-hour drive back home gave me ample time to absorb everything that had occurred the past couple of days. My mind wasn't set on one school yet, but I have to say that on first glance, SHU impressed me.

Less than a month later, I had to make my decision on which school I wanted to attend, but in the meantime, a couple of things happened.

First, about a week after the visit, Coach McCarthy at Albany called me and offered me $5,000 more, bringing my total scholarship per year up to $10,000. That night I talked to one of my friends from home, Rob Dim, who had played at Washington Township High School. He was also a current WR for SHU, and he gave me some advice: "Let Coach Bolis know that Albany offered more money and that if they are really interested in you, they need to match it." I really appreciated him telling me that, because at that point, I was feeling SHU a little more than Albany, but the money was looking funny to me. I took Rob's advice and made the call to Coach Bolis that night. I thought to myself, what did I have to lose? I mean, it was my future on the line here, so I had to treat it like business. I let Coach Bolis know the situation and told him that I was leaning toward SHU. However, the extra $5,000 could really seal the deal for me. He was on the road recruiting and would get back the following day to talk it over with Coach Gorham and the rest of the staff. After that, he said, he would call me with the verdict.

That following night, around six o'clock, Coach Bolis called me with the most disappointed-sounding voice. He said, "Gordon, I talked to Coach Gorham and let him know your situation, and he said he wants you to be a Pioneer, so he's going to give you the extra $5,000." I was relieved because the way he started talking initially, he sounded as if he had bad news. All in all, I was thrilled; that made my decision a lot easier. I was ready to go to SHU.

Prior to this conversation, I told my mom and dad that if I got that $5,000, I would be ready to commit. So when he told me I got it, I mumbled to Coach Bolis that I thought I was ready to commit. Coach Bolis told me to take a second to think about this decision and talk it over with my parents. So I told him I would call him back, and hung up. I talked it over with the family, and I felt it was the best decision for me. I got back on the phone and called Coach Bolis and told him I was ready to be a Pioneer. Instantly, Coach Bolis started screaming at the top of his lungs. Then he said he needed to pull over because he was on the road and didn't want to get in an accident since he was so excited. It was a great moment, and I'll never forget it. It felt as if a thousand pounds of pressure had been lifted off my shoulders with one phone call.

Remember though, my dream was always to make sure my parents would never have to pay for college, and I had failed. Even though I was happy about the opportunity, I was still upset that I had let them and myself down by not getting a full ride to a Division 1A school. All I ever wanted to do was be able to play as myself on the video game *NCAA Football*, and now I couldn't do that. Was I being selfish and not appreciative of this opportunity? Maybe. But I had a goal in mind, and I didn't fulfill it, and that's all I knew. Regardless, I was going to take advantage of and make the best of this opportunity.

To Coach McCarthy and Coach Ford from Albany, thank you so much for believing in me when no one else did. You will always have a special place in my heart (that sounds cheesy, but it is true).

The next day, Dim (Rob Dim, Dim is just what everyone calls him) called me and said he had Stephan Thomas standing right next to him. Stephan Thomas was the best player on the Egg Harbor Township Eagles, a team we had beaten that year. I knew he was a good player, and now that I was committed to SHU, I wanted him to commit there as well. So I gave him my best sales pitch and tried to convince him to come to SHU.

Finally, signing day was here, and I was proud to officially become a Pioneer. After all the paperwork, interviews, and pictures, I finally got to see who else had committed to SHU that year. To my surprise, I saw I wasn't the only South Jersey guy to commit. Along with me there were Sean Bell (Bishop Eustace, RB), Frank McConnell (Bishop Eustace, OL), Tim Goodwin (Holy Spirit, TE), Stephan Thomas (Egg Harbor Township, DB), and finally my high school teammate Pat Casey (Saint Joseph, LB). This group from South Jersey had the state on its back as we headed up to SHU in Fairfield, Connecticut, to leave our stamp.

The next day during gym class, I was playing basketball with my boy Phil. Coach Sacco was our gym teacher, and he pulled me to the side to introduce me to a coach from University of Buffalo. This was awkward, obviously, because I had signed my letter of intent the day before. Even with that being a done deal and my intention 100 percent set on going to SHU, this University of Buffalo coach still tried to persuade me to go to Buffalo. Not only did he say I could appeal the scholarship offer I accepted from SHU, but what he was doing also had to be somewhat, if not totally, illegal. Anyway, I told that coach I was happy with my decision and if he wanted to offer me a full ride, he should have done it a month ago.

Brother from Another Mother

Before I get into my college years, I feel it's important to introduce some important people in my life. My immediate family is definitely the most important group of people in my life, but the people I'm about to talk about are close runners-up.

The first family I'm going to introduce is the Valles family: Mr. Paul, Mrs. Pam, Andre, Hakeem, and Max. I first met the Valles family when I was about five years old during little league baseball season. Hakeem and I were on the same team, and we dominated. When everyone else on the team was playing just to get a participation trophy, we were trying to make sure we won every game. I think our competitive spirits are what made us friends in the beginning. Once we became close, our parents started to build their own relationships, and the rest is history.

When we were growing up, you could always catch us hanging out at each other's house. On random summer days, we'd have a barbecue in my backyard, and we would chill in the pool all day. Or I'd go over to the Valleses' house and play video games on a lazy Sunday afternoon. Regardless of where we were, we always had a great time. The times we had the most fun, in my opinion, were when we went on vacations together. Sometimes we would head to Orlando, Myrtle Beach, or our favorite location, Williamsburg, Virginia.

Every time we went on vacation together, we had a blast. We'd go-kart, fish, golf, and of course chill by the pool. It was definitely the good ol' days. We were kids with no cares in the world, just enjoying life. Those summer vacations were what made our families one because they gave us time to get to know one another. As I get older and grow as a person, I appreciate our relationship even more because the Valleses are people I can go to for anything, and vice versa.

The next family I want to introduce is the Ordille family: Mr. Paul, Mrs. Joanne, Andrew, Luke, and Rocco. I first got close to the Ordille family around sophomore year of high school when I met Andrew (the oldest son). Andrew is a year younger than I am, but I knew him because our high school was small and Andrew was also an athlete, so we knew each other through sports. That first year we met each other, we weren't that close, to be honest. Then, the following year (my junior year), we started to get to know each other a little bit more. It helped that we had a couple of mutual friends as well.

I think it was my relationship with Luke that really brought me close to the family. Andrew wasn't a football player, but Luke was, and that's how I got to know the rest of the family. Through football, Luke and I became close, and after I hung out at their house a couple of times with some of our teammates after school, it became a second home for me. While hanging out after school with the Ordilles, I got to know Mr. and Mrs. Ordille and found out they were really nice people. They give off such an admirable vibe; it's easy to be yourself around them, which I love.

The last family I want to introduce is the Earling family: Mr. Mike, Mrs. Tracy, Morgan, and Mike. I first interacted with the Earlings in high school as well. I met Morgan my sophomore year of high school. She's one year older than I am, but we had mutual friends, so we often were within the same circle. I got close with the Earling family through a son on the football team. Morgan's younger brother, Mike, played on the football team my junior year, and he was like a little brother to me. After summer football practices, I'd bring Mike home or even to Rodio's Diner, where Mrs. Earling would occasionally work. Before I knew it, I was hanging out with either Mike or Morgan all the time, and the rest is history.

All these families mean so much to me because they're my extended family. If I ever need anything from any of them, they're always there for me. There's a saying that I've always liked that defines my relationship with these families: "It doesn't matter who was there first. What matters is who came and never left your side."

I want to say to all of you I love you for everything you have done for me over the years—all the good times, the heart-to-hearts, the vacations, the positive vibes, the love, and the memories we have made together. I never forget how people make me feel, and what you all allowed me to do was be myself. For that, thank you.

Chicken Gordon Bleu

I think the date was August 4. That was when I left Jersey to start my next chapter in life up in Connecticut. The entire drive up there, I was filled with mixed emotions. My mom was sad but she was trying her best not to show it, and my dad was probably super excited since he was finally getting me out the house. It was a drive I'll never forget, because it was the start of something new.

Once we got to school and I was settled into my dorm room, it was time to say my good-byes. Instantly, my mom put on her sad but strong face as I gave her a hug. I could tell she wanted to cry, but surprisingly she didn't. My dad gave me a hug as well and told me what he tells me before every one of my football games: "Handle your business, and remember where you came from." After that, they hit the road. For about an hour, I just sat in my room, taking in the fact that they were gone. I think all college kids have a period when it connects with them that their parents aren't coming back for a while. It's a weird feeling, but you'll know what I'm talking about if you haven't gone through freshman year of college yet and plan to.

After three hours on the road, my dad called me to tell me they made it home safely. He also said that my mom started bawling her eyes out once they crossed the Tappan Zee Bridge. I knew she was going to let it out eventually. While on the phone with my pops, I headed up to the Pitt Center, which is Sacred Heart's athletic center. I went to check in with my coaches and be fitted for all my equipment in preparation for the start of camp the next day.

After getting everything I needed for the next day, I walked into the locker room for the first time with all my new teammates. It was cool meeting everyone, especially the guys in my class, because we'd be going through four years with one another. When I finally got to my locker, I was excited, but not for long; when I looked at my nameplate, I saw that they had spelled my name wrong. Instead of spelling my name Gordon Hill, it was spelled Gordan Hill. I was mad for about a minute, and then I let it go. I told myself that after my four years at this school, they'd never spell my name wrong again. The crazy part about it is that I didn't even want to ask to get it fixed. I wanted to walk into that locker room every day and use that as motivation and a reminder that I hadn't done anything there yet.

The next awkward situation involved the jersey sitting in my locker. See, I had been told I was going to play defense at SHU, but for some reason an offensive jersey was sitting in my locker. It was a red number 12 jersey, to be exact. Next to me was the other number 12 jersey, which was white and sat in QB Jamie Ross's locker. When we both noticed the apparent mistake, we switched jerseys.

The next day we got ready to hit the field for the first time as a team. I was so ready to show everyone what I could bring to the table as a freshman, and it was only a matter of time. As practice started, we got into our stretch lines and began warming up. As I began to do my high knees, Coach Bolis (my recruiting coach) started yelling at me about getting my knees up. If I remember correctly, he said, "Hill, these are called high knees, not low knees." From that point forward, I knew he'd always be hard on me. Or maybe that was just his way of introducing me to Sacred Heart football. Regardless, it was a memorable moment; it reminded me of how hard Coach Sacco was on me at Saint Joe.

Going into that first practice, I knew I was going to be third string on the depth chart because I was a freshman who hadn't proven himself yet. There were a senior named Zak Turner and a prep school transfer, Connor Candito, in front of me. Even though we were teammates, I came to practice and film every day with a mission. That mission was to make sure I took their spots before week 1 of the season. So what I did was simple: I just went out there and played the only way I knew how—fast and physical!

After a couple of practices, I began to adjust to the new playbook and new terminology. This allowed me to react faster and not think so much. After about two weeks of camp, I moved up to second string strong safety, and occasionally, I would get reps with the first-team defense. One practice, it rained extremely hard the entire time. The defense wasn't having the best day, and Coach Wiss was a little frustrated about how we were doing that day. I knew we had to make a play to change the attitude of the defense and, more importantly, end practice on a good note. So I thought, "Why not take it upon myself to make this change?"

The call was cover four, and I was lined up directly across from our big-play threat and senior tight end, Rich Rossi. The guy was a beast. The offense needed a big play, and I knew they were going to him, because they always did. After practicing with the team for about two weeks now and being observant, I had noticed Rich's favorite route was the seven cut. With that in mind, I assumed the seven cut was coming for sure. As the ball was snapped in the pouring rain, Rich ran straight toward me downfield. As he got to about ten yards, I knew he had only a couple of options left. He had to break left, right, or straight at me, but I knew that seven cut was coming. Just as I imagined, it was the seven cut, and I was ready for it. As Rossi made his move, I stared directly into the eyes of our QB, Tim Little, as he was about to release the ball. I was in perfect position to get an interception. Now all I had to do was make sure I didn't drop it. Fortunately, I caught the ball in the pouring rain and began running upfield, but after trying to make a move on the wet surface, I slipped. Although that interception didn't count for much, it was a big step in earning my coaches' trust, and it showed them I also had play-making ability.

The next day, before practice, Coach Wiss (just a reminder, he was my defensive coordinator) told me I'd be running with the first-team defense that day. I was a little surprised but ready at the same time. I had to lock in at practice because this would be my first opportunity to prove that I deserved to be a starter. Throughout that practice, I had one focus, and that was to be perfect at doing the little things—for example, lining up properly, disguising coverage, maintaining my leverage, and just being fundamentally sound. I wanted to make sure I controlled what I could control.

When that practice was over, I knew I had had a good day. I didn't make any mistakes, and I didn't have any missed assignments. The film that night solidified my assumptions, and I could tell my coach was impressed. Although I was having great days on the field, I could tell my coaches didn't want to build my head up with praise. I don't blame them though; I didn't really deserve any anyway. Honestly, I wasn't looking for a pat on the back. Playing time was all I needed.

After that day of running with the first team, Coach Wiss put me back at third string the next day. I didn't understand why he made me the backup's backup again, but I thought, "Whatever." I was playing well enough to start, so I thought for sure this had to be a test of some sort. That entire practice, I didn't get one rep of live action. I stretched in the beginning of practice and then sat on the sideline the entire time. I had conversations in my head that entire practice, wondering what could be the reasoning behind this move. I told myself, "This has to be a test. Just be cool." I consciously made sure I never exhibited any negative body language the entire practice. Really, I was too engaged in watching practice anyway. Once Coach blew his whistle to end practice, it was time for gassers. Since I hadn't exerted any energy the entire practice, I made sure I finished first every time.

The next day, while we were heading to the first film session, Coach Wiss pulled me to the side, and he had his serious face on. At first I thought he was mad at me, but I didn't know why. I was wondering, what had I done? Once he started talking, I realized what it was about. He was informing me that I would be the starter heading into week 1 of the season. I was overwhelmed with a sense of accomplishment, but I still had so much work to do. I mean, the first game of my college career hadn't even come yet. Before Coach Wiss could walk away, I asked him why he had decided to make me the starter. With a confused facial expression, Coach Wiss asked me, "What? Do you not want to be the starter?" I quickly said yes and began explaining where the question had come from. I told him, "I like to understand the reasoning behind people's actions. That's all." He said, "Because you play fast and physical and you just have fun out there." Then he walked away, which told me that the conversation was over.

With me solidified as the starter, I felt a little pressure on my shoulders. But it was good pressure, the type I look forward to. And I wasn't alone; I had a lot of help around me. Guys like Ahmad Covington, Chris Mandas, Justin Embler, Rueben McIntosh, and Paul Graziadei all made my job easier. The one who really took the time to make sure I was ready for this role as starter is one of my best friends, Alex Aitkens.

Alex was the free safety on the team and the one I would have to communicate with the most on the field. He was a kid from North Jersey who went to football powerhouse Saint Joseph Montvale. Basically, Al was the QB of the defense as a sophomore. He just knew where everyone needed to be at all times. He's the one who showed me the importance of film study and how to be a student of the game. He made sure I was always getting extra film study in. Even on the practice field, if he saw something I didn't do correctly, he'd let me know right away. Alex was my big brother and always looked out for me. He showed me the ropes and made sure I was prepared not only for this first game of my college career but for the rest of my career.

by Karyn Ochiuzzo

Before I forget, Al, I want to say thank you for everything you ever did for me. Thank you for being patient with me when I didn't understand things. Thanks for pushing me as a player. Thank you for reminding me to be humble and, more importantly, being a real-life example of how a good person carries himself. I know when you read this you're going to be shaking your head, saying some BS about how I don't have to say those things. But no, I do, because you were there to show me the right way to do things, and I appreciate that.

Before I knew it, camp was over, and the first game of my college career was here. It was a night game we hosted on Campus Field against the Marist Red Foxes. I never liked night games, because we didn't have lights at my high school field, so it was unfamiliar to me. Regardless, I had to deal with the bright lights. Of all the plays I was involved in that night, I still remember my first play ever on defense. We were in cover two, and I had Marist's number-one receiver to my side of the field. The ball was hiked, and in what seemed like just one second, Marist's receiver was almost beside me. For those who don't understand football, imagine standing fourteen yards away from someone, and in one second, while you're backpedaling, he's already crossed the fourteen yards to your original position, plus some. That's what happened to me on the first play of my college career. I was like a deer in headlights when I realized how much faster game speed was compared to practice. It felt as if everyone was in overdrive while I was still in cement, at least for that first drive. After that, I became more adjusted to the speed of the college game. I didn't really have a choice; I had to be.

That first game against Marist, we lost 20–7. I didn't think anything of it though, to be honest. See, in high school, I had a lot of influence on whether my team won or lost based on my performance, because I played both ways. In college, however, I played only one way, and I had to make sure I was accountable for my responsibility on each play. A lot of trust went into it, but I got used to it as I started to know my teammates. Since I wasn't playing offense and defense, I didn't feel as responsible for the loss as I would have in high school.

As the season continued, I became more and more adjusted to the college game. However, I still wasn't used to the demands of being a student athlete. I didn't have the balance down yet. Week after week, I was getting papers back with average grades on them. I was used to getting all As in high school, but my work wasn't up to par for the college level yet. It wasn't so much that I couldn't handle the work or that I wasn't smart; it was a matter of applying myself. I was putting football before my classwork, but I had a good reasoning behind it, or so I thought. See, I was the only freshman to start every game his freshman year. With that responsibility came hours of film study and a thorough understanding of the playbook and game plan that week. I didn't want to be OK at football. I wanted to be remembered wherever I played. With that idea in mind, many hours had to be put in. My social life suffered from it and, more importantly, my schoolwork. I'm not going to lie to you: I didn't try my hardest my freshman year in the classroom. I just made sure my grades were good enough to be eligible to play.

That freshman year, football season didn't turn out the way I wanted it to from a team perspective. We finished the year 5–6, and that was difficult for me after coming from such a winning program in high school. Individually, I was happy but not exactly satisfied with my progress. I had accomplished my goal of starting as a freshman, and I had grown as a player, but I had so much more to learn and improve on.

Like our team's record that year, my grades that first semester were a little below average. I finished the first semester with a 2.6 GPA. That's right, a 2.6. As I said earlier, I wasn't happy with my performance in the classroom, but the positive was that I knew what I had to change to do better.

When winter break was over, it was time to get serious about a couple of things. One, I needed to take school more seriously, and during spring semester, I was able to do that. Two, I wanted to become more knowledgeable about our defense. Three, I wanted to really get to know my teammates, because during the season I was so focused on myself that I almost didn't see anyone else. It sounds selfish, but it was true.

For those who don't know, during the off-season, if you want to call it that, college-football players have a lot more time on their hands. We had some early mornings during the spring, but once we got through our morning commitment to the team, we were pretty much free for the rest of the day.

The first phase of spring for a college-football player is winter workouts. In my opinion, winter workouts are the worst part of being a college-football player. It's a way to weed weak people out of the program and see who's serious about the game of football, in my opinion. My freshman year, winter workouts damn near killed me. They were rough, but I needed them. Every day during winter workouts, it felt like Coach Wiss would single me out when I got to his drill. He'd make sure I was giving my all, and if I wasn't, he'd let me know about it in front of everybody. I used to hate it, but I knew he meant well and was just trying to push me.

The next phase of spring for a college-football player is spring ball. To me, this is the fun part of spring because you get to hit somebody. The night before spring ball started, our freshman running back, Keshaudas Spence, and I talked about life for hours over a game of *NCAA Football* (the video game). We talked about our visions of the future and how we had to be important parts of the success of Sacred Heart football. We knew we were young, but we also knew what we had to offer. We didn't get done playing until about two thirty in the morning, knowing we had our first practice of spring ball in about three and half hours. Shaudy and I didn't care though; we were so excited to get back on the field after the previous season.

Nobody knows it, but that night Shaudy and I made a promise to each other that we would help turn the program around. It might sound silly, but my dorm room that night had the energy of an executive-level business meeting. And if you want, I guess you can say we were just negotiating. By the way, I beat Shaudy that night in *NCAA Football* 56–49.

With a couple of hours of sleep under our belts, Shaudy and I were the first two headed up to the Pitt Center in preparation for the first day of spring ball.

I don't want to go into spring ball, because I don't think it is that important to share with you. All you need to know is that Coach Wiss didn't treat me like a freshman anymore. After every mistake I made, he let me hear about it.

Also, just so I don't forget to cover this, I want to talk about the friendships I formed during that spring. I really got to know my teammates during that time. I was getting closer with people like Keshaudas Spence, whom I mentioned, Preston Sanford, Connor Candito, Stephan Thomas, Tim Goodwin, Kyle Church, and Dennis Reagan, to name a few. But you'll get to know more about them later.

Finally, I want to end this chapter by talking about someone who was very instrumental in my life, and that's Paul Graziadei. Paul was a senior when I was a freshman, and everyone used to call him Grandpa because he was the oldest dude on the team. I think he was a twenty-four-year-old senior. But in all seriousness, Graz was an important person to many of us, and he was especially important to me. He was the one who always looked out for everyone. Whether it was about on-field issues or off, he was the one you could talk to about anything.

Graz, I just want to say thank you for everything. Thank you for being a big brother, a mentor, and just a good person. I appreciate all the talks about life we had and all the wisdom you shared with me. Many people don't know what you did for others, because you did the real work behind the scenes. The people you helped, will never forget you. G, I think we got along so well because you were me from the future. I don't know whether that makes sense, but what I'm trying to say is that we're the same person. You know I could go on and on, but I just wanted to make sure I said thanks. Oh yeah, I know you remember those losses I used to give you in *NCAA Football*. Those were good times. Anyway, I love you, man. Thanks for everything.

Why Not Us?

After completing my freshman year of college and enjoying my time off with my family and friends back home, it was time to get back to work. All summer I was thinking about this season and the new opportunities ahead of us. But before I could immerse myself into the world of football, I had a prior commitment. That commitment was going through summer RA training (residential assistant).

RAs are first responders to the majority of the needs of students in student housing. About a week before all my other teammates came to campus, I was learning the ins and outs of this challenging position. And trust me: it's tough.

Once football camp hit, I had double duty. I'd go from practice to film, to RA meetings, to football meetings, and back to RA training sessions. I had a full schedule every single day for about two or three weeks. It was all worth it though. Football camp was rough for me that year, but it wasn't because of my busy schedule. It was because Coach Wiss's expectations of my performance everyday was higher. I could totally be doing my job on a play, but he expected excellence from me every play. He'd always remind me that I wasn't a freshman anymore. At one practice I got tired of hearing him singling me out. I hope I don't send the wrong message because Coach Wiss got on other people too, but that day I felt he was trying to test my mental state.

On that day, we did a crazy amount of conditioning, and I was tired of it. I was never one to complain about working out, but that day was an anomaly for me. We were doing one of Coach Wiss's infamous conditioning circuits, and I just snapped. In the middle of the circuit, I started making the most unwarranted comments about how I felt about the conditioning. I said, "This is some bullshit!" Looking back on it, I can see I was tripping.

After every comment I made, Coach made my teammates and I do more and more conditioning. Eventually, Coach Embler snapped at me and said, "Gordon, shut the f*** up!" I listened to Coach Embler because I could tell he wasn't playing. Also, I didn't want to kill my teammates; I knew they were tired from all the extra conditioning. Plus, I didn't want my teammates mad at me either, so it was in my best interest to chill. So I did.

I think Coach Wiss got a laugh out of it. His mind is so twisted; he would have had us doing conditioning for the entire practice if he could. I realized that I didn't have as much juice on the team as I thought I did. That was a good moment for me though, because I needed someone to check me. I was getting too comfortable and needed to shut up and chill. So Coach Wiss, thank you for putting my teammates and I through that. And Coach Embler, thank you for speaking some sense into my head, because you know Coach Wiss would have kept us going as long as he was allowed to.

After camp was over, it was time to start the season. Like every team in the nation, we were hopeful that this season was the one for us. Unfortunately, it wasn't. We started the season off with a four-overtime loss to Morgan State. After the loss, the energy and morale among the team were horrible. Teammates were talking behind other people's backs about how they weren't that good. The coaches didn't seem to bring the energy they once did. It felt as if people didn't care.

In a defensive backs meeting, Coach Wiss had one of the realest talks ever with us. Once everyone got into the room, he looked at all of us without saying a word. We sat there in silence for a little while. The mood of the room got serious, and we knew that what he was about to say was going to be real. He started by saying that when he yelled at us out on the field, it wasn't just to make us mad. The purpose of it was to help us understand that we had made a mistake and needed to fix it. If we, as a defensive back group, kept making mistakes out on the field, he could be fired. Our performance on game day could be the difference between him being able to and not being able to support his family financially. And to get serious with us, he mentioned the possibility of never seeing any of us ever again owing to his dismissal from the team. It sounds crazy that a college-football coach's job security lies on the backs of eighteen- to twenty-one-year-olds, but that's the truth.

After that conversation, everyone locked in during our film session. We needed to because we were playing a very good Colgate team that week. After a week of tough practices, we headed to upstate New York. But we should have never even stepped on the field with that team, because we didn't come to play that day, at least defensively. They had their way with us, and it was embarrassing. The worst part about it was the long ride back home to Connecticut.

I thought I had played well that game, but the next day, walking into the film room to get our grades, I learned otherwise. Coach Wiss wasn't happy at all with our performance, not only with the DB group but also with the defense as a whole. Coach Wiss didn't even have his mad face on that day. He had his disappointed look on instead.

As we had the previous two weeks, we lost again. We turned a bad situation into an even worse one. It felt as if everyone who was connected to the program had shut down.

Midway through my sophomore year, something none of us expected affected the team. Our head coach, Paul Gorham, got sick and was hospitalized. For the longest time, no one told the team what had happened or how long he was going to be out. Eventually, Coach Nof told us he would be stepping in as interim head coach while Coach Gorham recovered from his illness. It was a shock to us that Coach Gorham had gotten sick, and it threw us off.

The rest of the season was a waste. We were out there playing for our pride, pretty much. We finished the season 2–9, and I was utterly embarrassed to wear my Sacred Heart football hoodie around campus. The exit meeting we had as a whole team was about putting the entire season behind us and moving forward. Coach Nof also told us that he would become the new full-time head coach for the upcoming 2013 season.

After everyone came back to campus after winter break, it was time to get back to work. We had winter workouts and spring ball ahead of us, but for some reason, things felt different. I don't know exactly what it was, but the energy around the team was foreign. I don't think we knew whether it was a good or bad vibe yet, but we all felt it. Different things happening with the school also directly affected the team around this time. The biggest change was the hiring of Bobby Valentine as the school's athletic director. Also, Coach Nof was officially named our head coach from this point forward. The change that we loved the most (including me) was the new jerseys and gear we got. With all these changes, we felt we had a fresh start, and we were ready to reintroduce ourselves not only to the Northeast Conference but to the college-football world, period.

But a couple of new jerseys didn't mean we were going to win all of a sudden. We had to put the work in and grow as a team, and we knew that. That entire spring ball was an all-out war between our offense and defense. Now, when I say "war," I mean it. Every practice we would get into multiple fights. I don't know what exactly was sparking all that anger, but it was obvious that something was going on. A couple of fights were about personal issues between teammates, but not all the fights were about that. It got so bad in the middle of spring ball that we had all-out brawls right in the middle of the field. These practices were, honestly, some of the most unproductive practices I have been a part of. The division between the offense and defense affected the coaches as well. There were times they would curse one another out in the middle of practices. The worst part about all this was it was only the beginning.

What showed me that this beef between the offense and defense was real was the fact that this divide continued off the field and on campus. One time RJ Noel, our starting quarterback, came up to me and tried to say, "What's up?" and give me a handshake. I was still angry from practice earlier, and I put my hand behind my back, cursed RJ out, and told him to keep it moving, since he was on offense. That sounds crazy, but it really went down like that. It was so out of character for me, but it felt like the right thing to do at the time. After that incident, RJ didn't talk to me for the remainder of spring ball.

This may not make any sense, but I think that year of spring ball was important in terms of our development as a team. It's almost like when two brothers fight each other for the first time. After the fight, they respect each other, realize they're family, and protect each other from that day forward. That's how I looked at the whole situation. At the end of spring ball, we settled our differences, whether they were personal or not. I think that spring showed us we were fighters and the energy we used against one another was the same energy we needed against our real opponents.

Remember that Coach Nof had been named head coach just a couple of weeks prior to spring ball, and he was adjusting to the position. Just so you can understand a little more in depth, Coach Nof used to be a yeller. He was the coach we didn't want to make a mistake in front of. But that was when he was the middle linebackers coach. Now, as a head coach, he was still learning the position, almost as if he was an incoming freshman. So when we were doing all this fighting among ourselves, he had to be neutral when he addressed the team as a whole instead of being only defensive minded. By the way, if any current SHU players read this and think Coach Nof is lenient nowadays, don't get it twisted. Even though I think he's calmed down, that doesn't mean he won't snap on you if you're doing the wrong thing. Just an FYI.

After we got through the rough patches of spring ball, summer was upon us. Before we all left to go home, a big group of our starters made an agreement to come back up to school to train, work, and live together. See, at bigger D1A schools, like Alabama and Michigan, there isn't a problem getting kids to stay on campus during the summer to work out; it's almost not an option. But at our school, financial issues don't allow all of us to stay on campus and work out during the summer. So we had to find jobs either on campus or around campus to pay for housing and food (shout-out to my family over at the moving crew and residential life). We made sacrifices, but they were worth it, for sure.

The living situation was unique and very beneficial to my teammates and I. We were able to get suite-style housing, where we all lived with one another. This was important. It allowed us to get to know people we didn't normally talk to or even get along with for whatever reason. That summer allowed RJ and I to get to know each other better. About a month prior, I had cursed him out, and we didn't talk, and now we were always playing video games and hanging out together. This summer with my teammates was really the turning point for our team. It helped us build trust, and ultimately that trust transferred over to the field seamlessly.

After two months of six-in-the-morning workouts, living together, tons of video games, and surviving on ramen noodles and Chipotle, we were ready for the season. Before we all went home for a quick break before camp started, we had one of the realest conversations ever. A huge group of us were all in a suite playing video games. I forgot how the convo started exactly, but I remember Paul Link, one of our captains, speaking the truth. His message was that even though we were horrible in the past, it was the past. We knew the work we had put in all summer, and we each knew what the others could do on the field. He pleaded, "So what if they pick us last in the preseason poll again? That doesn't matter, those are just opinions. Let's just surprise everyone and win it all this year. Why not us?"

That night was one of the most memorable nights of my life. Even though they were just words, there was so much truth behind what Link was saying. We had put in the work. We had the talent. Shoot, we were tired of losing. So now it was just a matter of showing you.

NWTS

The first day I got back to campus in preparation for camp, I was told we had a new defensive backs coach named Coach Butterworth. I didn't know much about the guy except that he was a SHU alum and had a unique last name. After talking to Coach Nof and Coach Wiss about him, I learned he was the real deal. The first time I met Coach B was in Coach Wiss's office. When I first saw him, I thought, "This guy is our new DB coach? Oh Lord." Coach B was a five-foot-six white Irishman from South Shore. Not to mention, he was rocking some all-white low-top Air Force 1s that looked as if they'd been through World War I (no, the shoes didn't look that bad, but you know what I'm saying).

With all that being said though, my first impression was that he was knowledgeable of the position. Once we started talking about football, I knew we'd get along. During this first meeting, we talked about his plan for the DB group this year. He told me his background in coaching, and I found out that while he was at UMass, he had coached two guys from my hometown, safety Jeremy Miles and WR Julian Talley, whom I mentioned earlier. After getting to know each other a little, we talked about the plan he had for me. I assumed he had watched film of the previous year because he knew a lot about how I played. He told me that if I worked hard and listened to the little things he told me, I would be an All-American. It was cool to hear someone have confidence in my ability like that, so I nodded and continued to listen to him.

Coach B was a talker. On top of that, he talked fast, and sometimes he was hard to understand because of his strong Boston accent. Nonetheless,

I could tell he was passionate about coaching, and I loved that. But all this was just conversation; I was excited to see what he would bring to the field the next day when camp started.

When camp started and we finally hit the field as a full team again, it felt great. With that 2–9 season behind us, it was time to turn things around. Camp that year felt different for a couple of reasons. For one, the class I had come in with was now all juniors, and almost all of us were playing important starting roles on the team. Two, Coach Nof was starting this season off fresh as our new head coach. Third, my position group had a new coach, and not only was I excited about what Coach B had to offer, but all the DBs were. Last but not least was the new wardrobe we got for the upcoming season and the formal introduction of Coach Fee, our first-ever strength and conditioning coach. Big things were happening over at SHU.

Once camp got rolling a little, there were early signs that something special was brewing on Campus Field. The offense looked confident, and everyone was on the same page. Defensively, guys were flying around and making plays on the ball. It was awesome. From a defensive backs perspective, we had to learn new techniques that Coach B brought with him from UMass. At first they were unfamiliar to us, but after a couple of days, we adjusted to them and started adding our own swag.

Oh yeah, let me not forget this. This is important! I haven't really talked about how Coach B was on and off the field, but let me tell you about this guy. The first time we had film as a DB group, Coach B introduced himself to the entire group. He told us that since majority of us were upperclassmen, he was going to treat us as such. He told us what he expected from us and what to expect from him. What to expect from Coach B consisted of the following: Coach B was going to be hard on us at all times to get the very best out of us as players. For example, when I would get an interception in practice, Coach B would still yell at me because I hadn't taken my read steps properly. That may sound like overkill, but it wasn't; he stressed attention to detail, and I had no problem with that. Also, Coach B didn't take any back talk from anyone. If we wanted to have a dispute with him on or off the field, it had to be for a logical reason, or else he didn't want to hear it. Coach B was one of those coaches who would yell across the field at us if we did something wrong. However, he wouldn't just yell at us; he would curse us out in front of everybody. His personal favorite curse word was "motherf***er." He used that word pretty much every day.

Even though he was hard on us as a DB group, none of us could ever say Coach B wasn't fair or was disrespectful or didn't look out for us, because he always did. He's the type of guy you either love or hate, and if you hated him, he was totally OK with that. If you told him you didn't like him, he'd respond by saying, "Well, good. I don't like you either." What I loved about Coach B the most was how real he was. He would always keep it real with us, no matter what. Coach B is also one of those people whose naturally funny and he'd have us cracking up at all times of the day. It was refreshing to have a coach with a sense of humor around, because after the last two seasons, everyone was so tense. He helped everyone relax when he was around, even the other coaches. Don't get me wrong though; when it was time to lock in and put in some work on the practice field or in film, he knew how to flip the switch. All right, enough about Coach B; he's not that cool.

As camp was ending and our season opener was approaching, I reflected on how much the game had slowed down for me. It seemed as if I was a step ahead of everyone else on almost every play. Things were just clicking. I was excited to put my preparation to work, and our first game was just days away.

There were two people at SHU I would always talk to about life and football: Coach Gardner (QB coach) and Ben Batchelder, our athletic trainer. Two days before our first game, I went to Ben to have our weekly talk about what he saw out there on the practice field. Since our first game was coming up, he talked about camp as a whole and his observations. He said he loved the psyche of the team and was extremely happy with the way camp had gone for the team as a whole. Like everyone else on campus, Ben wanted to see what we could do against other opponents.

Really quick, I want to talk about Ben a little more, because he's an important person in my life.. I want y'all to understand that Ben is one of my day ones at SHU. Throughout my four years at SHU and even now, he's someone I can talk to about a lot, and he's like a big brother to me. By the way, Ben, sorry for bringing you into the story so late. You know it's all love.

Our first game of the season was finally here, and everyone was excited for the opportunity to start the season off strong. We opened up the season with the Marist Red Foxes. They were a solid team that always brought their best, so it was a great opportunity to test where we were as a unit. This game had more pressure and importance wrapped around it than most people knew. As a football program, we (Sacred Heart University) had lost eleven of the past season openers at that point. I don't know why the streak was that long, but that's what it was. This year we wanted to be the group that changed that, and we knew we were capable. This season opener was an away game, so we headed to Poughkeepsie, New York, to face Marist in a battle under the lights. I was mad this game was a night game, since I hated those, but I had to suck it up.

Once we got into the locker room, you could feel the nervous energy and excitement of my teammates. Here's a little insider: during pregame in the locker room, I might be the most relaxed person in the room. You can usually find me in the corner of the room by myself with my headphones in, listening to the calmest music in the world. I was never a guy who got amped up for games. I'd just try to get as calm as possible, even to the point where I'd start falling asleep right before kickoff. Ask any of my teammates; they'll tell you.

As we lined up to head out to the field, I started this tradition as a junior that I would do for the next two seasons. I didn't plan it; it just suddenly became part of my routine. I would line up and look back and see RJ (QB) and Shaudy (RB) and give them both a nod as I looked them in their eyes. This was my way of saying to them, "You ready?" They'd nod back, and then it was time to get to work.

As we ran onto the field for the first time in those new jerseys, in front of a packed Marist crowd, I felt at peace. I don't know how else to explain that moment, but that's definitely the best way. We were on offense first and ended the drive with a field goal knocked in by our kicker, Chris

Rogers. So now it was defense's turn to show what they could bring to the table. From the first snap on defense to the end of the half, defensively we were flying to the ball every time. It was amazing to watch and be a part of. We were getting stops at will, and Marist was starting to get a little frustrated. Going into halftime, we were up 16–7, and our coaches were happy with our performance so far but let us know we could do better. While we were in the locker room, a huge storm hit the area, and we had at least an hour-long delay.

When we finally got back out to the field for the second half, our offense went wild. With ten minutes left in the fourth quarter, our offense put thirty-seven points up on the scoreboard. The score not only gave our defense confidence but also gave us a little cushion to try some different things defensively. Coach Wiss was the type of defensive coordinator to try different plays so he could see how they looked on film. Also, if he had a lead like the one we had late in a game, he would let the young guys play to let them gain some experience.

The final score of the game was 37–21. We had finally broken the season-opener losing streak that had been haunting us all those years. That night, Marist had fireworks immediately after the game. So not only did we win, but I was also able to take in a fireworks display with my family and all my teammates.

After that Marist victory, we ended up going on a four-game winning streak, bringing us to 5–0 as a team. The buzz surrounding our team was something we never witnessed before, because we'd never played that well. We started to get national attention from websites like FCSInsider.com. Even the Northeast Conference media and communications department started to show us a little more love. My teammates and I were doing Google Hangouts with Ralph Ventre, the director of communications and social media for the conference. People were interested in knowing what had changed in the program. What had sparked this tremendous start? Open and honest communication on and off the field was the answer. The biggest change I noticed after all the winning was how my teammates and I were treated and looked at by our classmates, our professors, and the administration. We gained a little respect, and it was obvious. Along the way, we gained some bandwagon fans, yet a couple of people on our own campus still doubted us. We didn't mind it though; it added fuel to the fire.

As we were going through this winning streak, I sat back at times and watched how everyone on the team interacted with one another. I noticed how happy everyone was. I saw teammates who never spoke to one another before say hi as they passed in the hallways of the Pitt Center. The coaches even interacted with the players a little bit more than they did back when we were 2–9 the season before. People were more laid back and gave off great energy. This positive energy didn't stop with the football team; I could feel it radiating all over campus. It was contagious! I was quite appreciative to finally see that here at SHU, because I had never seen it before.

Not only was football going well for me personally, but also my relationships with people I loved and the people I interacted with every day were in great standing. I was in a really good place. Monday of week 6 of the season, I was in Coach Gardner and Coach Gunningsmith's office having my weekly football/life talk. Coach Gardner was one of those people I could talk to about anything. Even now-a-days we'll occasionally catch up with each other and just talk about life. Since he's the same age as my sister Tiffany, I look at him as an older brother now that he isn't my coach. On that day, we talked about the state of the team and how we'd both seen changes. Most changes were positive, but we agreed that it seemed the winning, attention, and praise were beginning to get to some of my teammates' heads. It was inevitable, but as we were heading into conference play, we needed to throw that mind-set out fast, or we'd get humbled really quick.

Just as Coach G and I had talked about, Wagner College came to our field and handed us our first loss of the season. It was a 23–20 victory for Wagner with a last-second field goal allowing them to secure the win. What hurt my teammates the most was the fact that Wagner had entered the game with a 1–4 record. Not only were we the talk of the town, but we were playing a team with one of the worst records in our conference heading into the game. It was a trap game for us in a sense. They had nothing to lose, and as a team, we went into that game thinking it would be a walk in the park. Personally, I knew the game would be tough. They had Dom Williams at running back, a product of South Jersey and a great player. Defensively, they had athletes all over the place. I think they had a rough start to the season because they had a tough schedule early on. Wagner showed us that any given day, regardless of record, anyone can be beat. That's why you play the game.

Defensively, we didn't play our best game, and Coach Wiss was a little upset. I think there were even things he wished he had done differently heading into that game to prepare us. But Coach, at the end of the day, we're the ones who have to execute on the field, not you, so that one was on us. The loss was a shocker to everyone. We didn't expect to lose; we had gotten accustomed to winning. Throughout the conference, people started to say that our 5–0 start was a fluke and we weren't the real deal. I get why they would say that, but it was one game. This is college football, and it's hard to win them all.

The next week, we were playing our state rival: the Central Connecticut State Blue Devils. This was always a big game for us because it gave the winner bragging rights for best in conference from Connecticut. That entire week, newspapers from all over Connecticut and New York came to practice to build a story behind the game. The big question everyone had for our team was, did we think Wagner had exposed us, and could we bounce back from that loss? That week I had to answer those questions at least ten times, and my answer was always the same: the Wagner loss was the best thing that could've happened to us. We needed to be humbled.

Heading into the Central game, Coach Wiss really stressed the importance of slowing down Central's go-to guy, Rob Holliman. Rob Holliman was a small guy, but the guy was a baller and made plays from all over the field. He was an All-American, and when it came to all-purpose yards, the guy dominated. If we could stop him, we 'd feel pretty confident.

To start the game, our offense came out hot. It seemed as if every play we ran was successful. On the ground, Shaudy couldn't be stopped, and because of him, the play-action pass opened up beautifully. So you know RJ and Dube connected a couple of times. Quick sidenote: I don't think I explained how dominant Tyler Dube was at WR for us. Please understand, this dude was the best WR I ever played with or against. If you saw him on the street, you'd never know how skilled he was. Once you saw him on the field though, you would be amazed by the plays he made. Most people don't even know that he was a walk-on. I guess our coaches were wrong about him, but they learned quickly. The guy is a legend, and I'll leave it at that.

With twelve minutes left in the second quarter, we were up on Central Connecticut 28–6. We got comfortable on both sides of the ball. Suddenly, we looked up, and the score was 28–19, and Central had slowly crept back into the game as we were getting closer to halftime. After the half, Rob Holliman and the athletic line he ran behind started to wear out our defense. It seemed as if no matter what we did, he was going to get his yards. Our offense turned it back on in the second half and gave us some breathing room. Defensively, we held them off for the remainder of the game, but it wasn't pretty. The final score ended up being a 59–36 victory for us. We were happy we won, but Coach Wiss wasn't happy with our performance on defense. (To everyone on the offense who had career days that game, thank you for bailing us out; we needed you.)

When we watched the film the next day as a defense, Coach Wiss ripped our performance apart. It almost felt as if we had lost the game. I understood why he was frustrated and why he was stressing the importance of the mistakes we were making though. We were heading into the toughest part of our schedule, and he wanted to address simple mistakes that could be fixed but needed some addressing. As I said earlier, Coach Wiss never wanted or even allowed us to get complacent.

The next week, we played Bryant University. Unfortunately, they ran into our motivated defense and our offense that was on fire. We left Smithfield, Rhode Island, that day with a 56–28 victory. The following week we headed to Loretto, Pennsylvania, to play the Saint Francis Red Flash. For some reason, it was tough to go to Loretto and leave with a victory. I don't know whether it was the long trip out there to the middle of Pennsylvania or what. But I do know that it was always extremely hard to beat Saint Francis when they were playing at home. So you can guess that we lost out there again.

At 7–2, Coach Nof sat our team down and addressed the position we were in. We were having a great season up to this point, but our goal was to win the conference first, then look to the future. We had three games left, and Coach Nof told us we had to win these next three games to put ourselves in position for postseason play and to win a conference championship. So we locked in.

First was SHU versus Monmouth, 24–21 W.

Next was SHU versus Duquesne, 10–0 W.

Finally, we had our last game of the season in a suburb outside of Pittsburgh called Moon, Pennsylvania, where we played Robert Morris University for the conference championship. It sounds cliché, but everything we had worked for all summer and preseason was right there in front of us. When we got to the locker room, everyone looked locked in. There wasn't too much discussion or eye contact between teammates. Everyone was in his own zone. I went out for my usual pregame jog and stretch, and when I got back, I got dressed for the game.

Before we headed out to the field, Coach Wiss called the entire defense into a secluded part of the locker room. A couple of us sat in seats right next to Coach Wiss, while others stood over us, creating a dome-like effect. I was sitting right next to Coach Wiss, and so was my brother Connor Candito. Coach Wiss told us that this was it, this could be our last opportunity ever to play together as a group, and we'd never get this opportunity again. He looked at Connor, Troy Moore, and me and said, "We need great games from all of you if we're going to win today."

I looked Connor dead in the eyes, and he started to tear up. I became emotional too. I don't know why we both started to cry, but I think it was just the magnitude of the moment. Maybe it was the fact that this could be the last time we all played together. Maybe it was the realization that we had an opportunity to fulfill our goal. I can't explain it, but it was a moment I'll never forget. As the team began to leave the locker room to hit the field,

I sat there by myself for a couple more minutes just to get my mind right and to get my thoughts together.

When I finally hit the field, I was in a weird place. I had my emotions under control, and I was very calm, but I had so much anger inside of me. At least that's what it felt like. When we finally got on defense, I was ready to hit somebody. On the second play of the drive, their quarterback, Paul Jones, dropped back, saw nothing, and began to scramble. Like a missile, I sprinted directly toward him and hit that man with everything I had. After that hit, I finally felt I could settle into the game. We had made some great plays defensively to put our offense in great field position, which allowed us to go into halftime up 14–3.

Right out of the gate, we scored again in the second half, putting us up 21–3 in the third quarter. RMU never gave up though; they battled us all the way to the end, closing the margin to ten points late in the fourth quarter. After we ran back an onside kick for a TD, we knew we had the game locked up with the lead now 42–25. After getting a couple of stops on defense, RMU finally ran out of time, and we were NEC champs! We were headed to the national playoffs for the first time ever in school history!

Everyone stormed the field in excitement and started hugging one another. It was one of those championship moments. I was excited for everyone. Our hard work had finally paid off. Coach Nof was smiling from cheek to cheek, running all over the field. It was amazing. We did it. As all this was going on, I was standing still, taking in everything. My teammates were coming up to me and jumping on my helmet. It was awesome.

After the NEC Football Championship trophy was handed to Coach Nof, my teammates went wild with excitement. Out of the corner of my eye, I saw one of my teammates jump up and knock over a lady by accident. I picked her up as she adjusted her glasses. She said, "Thank you, and congratulations." A couple of months later, I found out that the woman I helped up was actually the commissioner of the Northeast Conference, Ms. Noreen Morris. So yeah, that was the first time we met.

After everything settled down a little, I got to celebrate the win with my parents and grandma. Oh yeah, I want y'all to know that my grandma has been to every one of my games. She's been holding me down since my first little league game, so thank you Grandma, for always coming to support me. To my cousins who also played sports, I'm sorry Grandma always came to my games, but we needed her; she was our good-luck charm.

When we got back to school, everyone congratulated us. What I was the happiest about was the fact that we had called this way back in the summer. We had talked about how we were going to surprise everyone and show them that we could do this, and we did it.

The FCS playoff selection show was next on our agenda, and it was quite an event. Here, we found out whom we were going to play in the first round of the playoffs, and we were matched up with Fordham University Rams. No more than three minutes after we found out whom we were going to play, Coach Wiss was already watching film and scheming for the game. I can guarantee you he watched film all night long to put us in great positions to be successful.

That week of preparation was amplified because, one, we were on Thanksgiving break, and two, this was the biggest game of our lives up to this point. Fordham had some ballers on offense. All three of their WRs were good, and they had an excellent QB who had transferred from UConn. Their tight end was also a beast and was probably the best tight end I've ever matched up against. To sum it up, they were an offensive machine with head coach Joe Moorhead at the controls.

Heading into the game, my biggest concern was that we didn't have any experience playing on this stage. I didn't want my teammates to be intimidated. I wanted us to play to our capabilities. The crowd that night was incredible. It was a packed house, and it felt as if we were playing in front of one hundred thousand people, even though it may have only been eight to ten thousand. Regardless, they were extremely loud from the start. Early in the first quarter, we got out to an early 7–3 lead after Shaudy broke off an amazing sixty-five-yard TD run. Keshaudas Spence, a.k.a. Shaudy, was our running back who carried the team on his back all season long. He was our spark plug on offense, and as he went, we went as a team. He brought so much passion to the game, sometimes a little too much, but I didn't mind it. It just showed me that he cared. A lot.

After we took that early lead, Fordham slowly took control of the game, and we never recovered. We lost 27–37, and our season was over, but I was so proud of my team. I got to see my teammates grow as players and people. I saw relationships with friends becoming stronger. Most importantly, I saw and was a part of a football culture at SHU that was turning into something beautiful. That loss to Fordham sucked, but so much good came from that season that it didn't even matter to me. I was so happy for our seniors, like Alex Aitkens, Greg Moore, and Paul Link. They saw where the program was when they got to SHU, and to leave in that manner was probably a great feeling. So thank you to all the guys who were part of that team, especially the senior class. I appreciate y'all and what you've helped build at SHU.

Although some guys graduated, we had a great foundation returning for next season. Yeah, we were happy with our season, but now we wanted to improve and do even better next year. And trust me: making it to the playoffs and getting a taste of success only made us hungrier.

SAY WHAT'S REAL

After reading and writing the previous three chapters, I want to do this one a little differently. I feel I was repetitive in the last chapter, so I'm going to switch it up because I was getting bored. Hopefully, you weren't though, and if you're still with me, I appreciate it.

This chapter is about my senior year, if you didn't guess already. To those who enjoyed all the talk about football in the book, I'm sorry, because it's pretty much over. To sum it up, we won the conference championship after a 9–2 regular season and played Fordham in the playoffs again. We lost, but let me tell you everything that happened behind the scenes from my team's and my personal perspectives.

This chapter starts in Panama City, Florida, during spring break. Keshaudas, Preston, Kyle, Connor, Kellen, Tino, and I went down there to enjoy our last spring break of college. We had just dominated our last winter conditioning at SHU, so this trip was our celebration. We were having a great time, but something that threw us all off was a phone call we got in the middle of our trip from Coach Edwards, our defensive line coach. He wasn't just a coach to some of us; he was more like a big brother we could go to for advice.

When he called Keshaudas, it was to tell all of us that he would be leaving SHU and begin coaching at Fordham University. At first it shocked us all, because we had just lost to Fordham in the playoffs a couple of months ago. After the initial shock of the news wore off, we came to terms with his decision. He further explained why he made the move, and after hearing him out, we understood why it was necessary. There were never any hard feelings toward him from any of the players; it was all love. We wanted the best for him and his future. He told us we could always call him if we ever needed anything, and if you know him personally, you know he wasn't saying that just to say it.

The rest of the trip down in Panama City was fun, but in the back of everyone's mind was Coach Edwards. We'd be out as a group, and out of nowhere someone would just say, "Damn, Coach Edwards really left." It was as if we didn't want to believe it.

When we got back to campus for spring ball, there was a new coach on the staff. Before I met him, I was told he was from the same coaching tree as Coach Edwards and was not only a very good player but also very smart. His name was Coach Cooke, and when I first met him, I thought to myself, "He ain't no Coach Edwards." However, what I liked about Coach Cooke, was that he didn't try to be Coach Edwards when he first got around the team. He was his own person, and I think that made his transition to SHU easy for both parties. Yeah, he may have been a youthful spin-off version of Coach Edwards, but he stayed true to himself, and I respected that.

The next obstacle we ran into during summer workouts wasn't an obstacle the whole team knew about. But, it was something I felt needed addressing. That may sound selfish, but trust me: it was important. The issue I'm talking about was regarding RJ, our QB. He was now entering his second year as a starter and was coming off a record-breaking season. As a redshirt freshman, RJ dominated the Northeast Conference and led us to our first NCAA playoffs appearance. With all that success coming at him so fast and at a young age, I began to see signs that it was all going to his head. If you asked him, he'd probably have told you otherwise, but it was obvious. One thing that didn't help the situation was the media and people on campus. Not only did RJ start feeling himself, but people also started calling him RJ Football, after the nickname Johnny Football, referring to Johnny Manziel. It was weird though, because no one wanted to say anything, even the coaches.

So I took it upon myself to do something. I decided to live with RJ for two months during summer workouts. I don't want to make it sound as if I lived with RJ only to monitor his mind-set and keep him humble, because it wasn't like that. At this point, RJ and I were good friends, and we decided that it would be awesome to live together. In the most respectful way possible, some nights I would talk to him about his success and give him subtle reminders to stay humble. One night we talked about the progression of his name in the conference. At first, people never pronounced his name right. They would always say "RJ Nole." Then after a couple of wins and a couple of interviews, they started to get his last name right and actually say "Noel" properly. After the season and all the success, that's when the RJ Football thing came about. I stressed to him that I wanted "RJ Nole" back. That RJ was so humble and hungry and kept his head down and worked. That RJ had a chip on his shoulder and something to prove. I wanted that back. I'll never know completely, but I think he got the message.

When camp started my senior year, I was completely in a teaching role. I took everything I learned from my coaches, my brother-in-law, Graz, Alex, and Ahmad, and I shared it with all the young guys as much as I could. That preseason I had a talk with Coach Wiss. We talked about my role on the defense and how he wanted to put more responsibility on me. We talked about different schemes and even somewhat of a position change for me on third downs. I was a little unsure of what he had in mind, but he kept reminding me that I'd be in great positions to make plays. I knew he had my best interest in mind, so I was all for it, especially if it could help the team.

When the coaches' preseason poll for our conference came out, we were picked first. It was cool to get respect from our peers, but at the same time, it put a target on our back. Our coaches constantly reminded us that preseason polls mean nothing, and they were right. You still had to play the games, and if anyone knew that, it was us.

After our 3–0 start, Coach Butterworth told me he wanted to talk to me after film. Coach B was rarely in a serious mood, so when he was, we knew it was important, and this was one of those times. With just him and I in the room, Coach B asked me one of the realest questions anyone has ever asked me. He said, "Gordon, do you really love football?" His question threw me in shock. I froze up and then started to tear up, but I didn't understand why I was getting emotional. Coach B explained that the question came about because of my performance in last week's game. We had played the Division 2 team from Assumption College, and he felt I was just going through the motions—and you know what? I was. Why was I? Maybe because they were D2 and we were huge favorites to win, so I got complacent. I don't know what to say other than that, but I agree that that game was the least impressive performance of my career. The sad part was that on film, it looked as if I was OK with being average, and that's not OK. That's why we were having this meeting, and that's why this question was asked.

After fighting back tears, I told Coach B that I did love football, which is true. The thing I appreciate most about that conversation is that Coach B cared enough about me to intervene and ask the tough question. He didn't have to do that, but he did and made sure I wasn't OK with being just OK. Looking back on it, I think those tears I was holding back were really tears of happiness, happiness that came from someone caring, and for that, Coach B, thanks again. I seriously needed that.

Two games later, we played the University of Delaware. This was the biggest game in our school's history to date. It was little Sacred Heart against CAA powerhouse Delaware. All week heading into the game, we kept hearing about how good they were and how we were double-digit underdogs. Well, we won that game 10–7 in one of the best games I've ever been a part of. To the coaches at Delaware, you made me play the way I played against you. You guys never offered me, and I was right in your backyard, so this was karma getting back to you. To Jerel Harrison and especially Diante Cherry, thank you for talking trash that game. Y'all were great motivators. Diante Cherry, I'll never forget what you said to me on the first play of the game: there was no point in actually trying since you were going to blow us out anyway, right? It was funny when you didn't have anything to say to me at the end of the game. I hope you learned from that experience and humbled yourself a little, because you're actually a good player. Good luck in the future with football and all your other endeavors.

To my bro Tyler Dube, thank you so much for making that game-winning catch against Duquesne. That was so clutch. RJ, great decision, man. You two kept our season alive with that completion.

I want to thank Saint Francis for coming to our field and beating us 30–27 in a nail-biter. You guys always brought your A game against us and kept us on our toes. We appreciated that as a team because you were always a reminder that we had to come correct regardless of records. After the loss to Saint Francis, our whole team went into playoff mode. We had to because if we lost one more game, we would lose control of our own destiny when it came to the playoffs.

To the Bryant Bulldogs, you guys were having one hell of a season. It was fun to watch you guys make your run. I'd always walk into Coach Gardner's office and throw on some film of not only your offense but your defense as well. I really enjoyed how you guys played that year. What I didn't understand though, was why a couple of your teammates posted an Instagram picture claiming you guys had the conference won already. In the caption, there was even a mention of rings and stuff like that. The interesting part was that you still had to play us and Wagner, who ended up beating you as well. All I'm saying is, why add fuel to the fire if you don't have to? Trust me: we hung that Instagram picture up all throughout our facility that week. It was just the reminder we needed. I guess what I'm saying is just be humble men, and then stunt after you get the rings—that's all.

Another thing people don't know is that Stephan, one of our corners, poked me in my eye before our playoff game against Fordham. It was the biggest game of our careers, and as we did every game, Stephan, JD, and I went out to the field to warm up a little. We did our usual lap and stretch, and we finished with some half-speed one-on-one drills. This time, however, as I was in the WR role, Steph poked me in the eye hard enough to make my eye completely close. So while my team was out warming up for the game, I was in the locker room with Ben, Jess, and Dr. Redler, trying to get my eye to open. Once it was time to hit the field as a team, I had to open my eye; I had double vision. For a second, I panicked because I didn't think I could play like that, but I did, and I had arguably the best game of my life. As I said earlier, we lost, but at the end of the day, I had a great time balling with my boys one last time.

I think the biggest lesson I learned my senior year was to be humble not only as a football player but also as a person in general. There was a play I'll never forget from my senior year, and it happened during our season opener against Marist. It was the first snap of the second half, and I was at safety. My bro John Snee was at Mike linebacker, and Marist came out in a three-by-one set. On that play, pre-snap, I told John to strictly play the pass and forget about the run. Call it a hunch or whatever, but I had a good idea of what they were running. A second later, the ball was snapped. I wasn't sure whether he fully heard what I said, but Johns' actions showed me he got it. John played the WR exactly how I wanted him to, and because of that, he made the QB overthrow his intended WR. I intercepted the pass and ran it back for a TD.

Now, the point of this is that I realized I didn't really make that play. So many things had to go right for me to be in position to make that play. For one, John had to play the WR perfectly, which he did. Thanks, John. Two, Coach Wiss had to call the play that put me in the position to possibly catch the interception. Three, my other teammates had to cover their men well enough to make the QB not want to throw their way. So my point is I didn't make that play myself; I was just a small piece of the puzzle.

A friend of mine named Christian Dudzik composed a tweet that read, "I will continue to say it—individual awards are silly in football. Individuals could not be successful without the other 10 on the field. Furthermore, the 11 on the field could not be successful without good coaches and a good support system in place. Awards are media fiction."

I think he summed up what I learned that year. Be humble, because it's not all about you. In football and in life, we need one another to be successful. You can't do it all on your own. So say thank those people who assist you on the way to your goals, appreciate what they've done for you, and never forget them.

So that was it. As far as college football goes, my career was over as a Pioneer. Yeah, I didn't fulfill my goal of getting SHU onto ESPN or

ESPN2 as we, hopefully, made a run deep into the playoffs. But I know my teammates and I left the program and school in better condition than when we first got there. More importantly, I created some of the best relationships with some of the coolest people I've ever met, and for that, I'm thankful.

Open Letter

After college, I pursued the NFL, which took me to North Gwinnett, Georgia, for training. I was there for two months and went through some of the most physically and mentally challenging workouts in my life. In the end, it taught me a lot about myself. For one, it showed me that I really loved the game of football. More importantly, it showed me how to push myself past my mental limits.

Throughout the process, I remember thinking about all the guys from South Jersey who followed their passion to the pro level. One day, we had one of the hardest workouts I've ever been through, and I needed some additional motivation. For some reason, the first person that came to mind was South Jersey native Joe Gatto. Joe is younger than I am and is currently a pitcher with the Los Angeles Angels of Anaheim's organization. I thought to myself, "At eighteen years old, Joe was thrown into this lifestyle, so at twenty-one, I know I'll survive." Thank you, Joe. I was leaning on you that day.

After training, pro days, and the draft were over, I was headed to San Diego, California, to be a Charger. I was excited for the opportunity and for everything I was going to learn in this chapter of my life. I had finished school; I was far from home and out there by myself. My dad kept making the joke that he was just happy I had gotten my first legit job. He was right though; it pretty much was. While I was in San Diego, I played with and learned from some of the greats. Guys like Eric Weddle, Brandon Flowers, and Darrell Stuckey were always around to help me when I had a question.

It was a blessing being able to pick their brains about not only football but life as well.

Anyway, everything was going great until week 2 of the preseason against the Arizona Cardinals. I injured my left knee, which sidelined me for a while. It was a freak accident, but you know what? That's life. I wasn't going to stress over something like that. I kept working and reminded myself to go with the flow.

After six weeks of rehab, my knee was feeling good to go. Unfortunately, the Chargers released me. But I'm extremely thankful for the opportunity they gave me. Also, I'm appreciative of my time with the Chargers because I learned so much and had some great experiences with some really cool people. I want to thank Craig Mager, Kyle Emanuel, Adrian Phillips, Curtis Grant, and Ryan Mueller for being good people and always looking out for me. I appreciate you guys, and I wish you the best in the future. I know you will all be extremely successful.

Once I got home, I began working out with my high school team to stay prepared for a workout that was coming up. After a couple of days though, my knee started acting up again, and it was time for surgery. The craziest part about the day of surgery was my agent calling me to let me know the Kansas City Chiefs wanted to bring me in for a workout. It was good that teams were still interested in me, but the timing couldn't have been worse. That's life though.

After surgery, I found myself sitting on the couch in my house for three days straight because I could barely bend my knee. I was bored doing nothing, and I wanted to challenge myself in some way. Writing this book was that challenge. I had all this time on my hands, so I thought, "Why not?" I started writing, and this is what came about. I was talking to my cousin Courtland, and he said something interesting to me after I mentioned to him that I had started writing a book. He said, "Gordon, all your life you've been challenged physically through the sport of football. Now that it has been taken away from you for a brief period, you have to challenge yourself in other ways. You may have always had the urge to do something like write a book. However, because of football, you never had to tap into this intellectual side of yourself to feel challenged. This is that opportunity." Courtland was so right, and I loved the way he articulated what he saw me doing through this book.

At the current moment, I'm completely healthy and ready to get back on the field if that opportunity comes knocking. In the meantime, I'm just going to live my life, and whatever I end up doing, just know I'm going to have fun doing it.

Even though I have talked about my life and some of the experiences I went through, I really wanted to talk about the people I have met in my life so far. I am so thankful for all of you, because you've all helped shape my life and helped me along the way, whether you know it or not. So thank you again, and I want to let you know that this book is for all of you.

About The Author

Gordon Hill is a professional football player. He briefly played for the San Diego Chargers and is now busy pursuing his other passions.

Hill was born in Sicklerville, New Jersey. He attended Saint Joseph High School in Hammonton, New Jersey, and Sacred Heart University in Fairfield, Connecticut. At Sacred Heart, he was a four-year starter on the football team and formally played safety. Hill was named captain, all-conference, and all-American. While attending college, he also worked as a residential life assistant.

The Credits

I want to dedicate this chapter to all the people who are important to me but weren't mentioned in the book. I hope you understand I couldn't talk about everyone individually; however, you are significant to me. Thank you to all of you for everything you've done for me.

Rahim Abdullah
Dylan Ackerson
Mike Adams
Corie Adamucci
Derek Adamucci
Kellie Adamucci
Rick Adamucci
Ross Adamucci
Alex Aitkens
Uwem Akpanikat
Ashton Alicea
Narci Reed Alwan
Jarret Alwan
Chi Chi Ariguzo
Ryan Arroyo
Delvon Artis
Manny Asprilla

Mike Austin
Rasheed Bailey
Ronald Duke Baines
Frank Bakirtzis
Tre Banks
Joe Barbar
Jordan Barbone
Andre Barboza
Tom Barcia
Rashad Barksdale
Byron Barney
Erin Barry
Kevin Barry
Dolores Barry
Nick Bartoli
Arne Baruca
Ashley Batchelder

Ben Batchelder
Devon Bateman
AJ Baxter
Tyler Beauchesne
Sam Belkin
Sean Bell
Carma Belton
William Belton Sr.
William Belton Jr.
Nicholas Benza
David Berment
Ashley Betanski
Gillian Bianchi
Rhonda Bianchini
Jarred Bianchini
John Binford
Jackie Bockarie
Todd Bockarie
Connor Bohl
Kevin Bolis
Shaun Bowman
Brian Bradley
Elizabeth Bradley
James Bradley
Sean Bradley
Tara Bradley
Owen Bradley
Courtland Bragg
Jarret Bragg
Gawain Bragg
Gabby Bragg
Gawain Bragg Jr.
Vinny Branchini

Dave Bray
Ryan Breen
Alexader Bright
Andrew Brigley
Terry Briscoe
Leon Briscoe
Buddy Brown
Matthew Brunick
David Bruno
George Buahin
Jordan Burroughs
John Bushell
Stephanie Buslovich
Jackie Butterworth
Bryan Butterworth
Kenny Byram
Damiere Byrd
Ryan Byrne
Kenny Byrum
Charles Cade
Anthony Calabrese
Billy Caldwell
Juanita Caldwell
Pete Callaghan
Caleb Camacho
Blake Campbell
Jeff Campbell
Donna Candito
Connor Candito
Nick Candito
Kaitlyn Carman
Colin Carney
Tykera Carter

Devon Carter
Sonia Casey
Pat Casey
Bill Casey
Joy Casey
Ben Castellano
Michael Castellano
Matt Castronuova
Connor Caveney
Jessica Cerrato
Jake Chamseddine
Breonna Chandler
Ed Charlton Jr.
Nate Chavious
Jawon Chisholm
Kyle Church
Sean Clark
Stephen Clement
Mark Clements
Jess Colborne
Garry Coles
Meghan Collins
Rob Coloney
Matt Colucci
Dave Comerford
Colleen Connolly
Lamisha Cook
Mike Cooke
Chelsey Corbo
Jack Corcoran
Ryan Cottrell
Shanae Covington
Sylvia Covington

Denise Covington
Raheem Covington
Aneesah Covington
Kyle Covington
Ahmad Covington
Ayanna Covington
Karl Covington
Jack Coyne
Dave Crescenzo
Allie Crescenzo
Nick Crescenzo
PJ Cronin
Jay Croom
Matt D'Attile
PJ Dailey
Nesrin Danan
Dr. Susi David
Billy Davis
Jake Davis
Kia Marie Dawkins
Anthony De Rosa
Dan Deal
Maureen Dean
Gary Deanley
John DeMarco
Maureen DeMarco
Megan DeMarco
Anthony DeRosa
Paul DeRose
Tyreiq DeShields
Kristina Desrosiers
Jaylin Deveau
Michael Dias

Francis DiGiorgi
Matthew DiGrazio
Scott Dillman
Robert Dim
Kate Doctor
Jack Donio
Connor Donnelly
Nick Doscher
Dot
Sean Dougherty
Liam Doyle
Tyler Dube
Ethan DuBois
Christian Dudzik
Kevin Duke
Cole Duncan
Andrew Durkin
Danielle Durso
Matthew Easterday
Bob Earling
Evan Earling
Grace Earling
Jenna Earling
Jerry Earling
Kelly Earling
Michael Scott Earling
Michael Earling
Morgan Earling
Tracy Earling
Michael Eaton
Darin Edwards
Ben Eedle
Peter Elliott

Kyle Emanuel
Justin Embler
Kristin Emerick
Diane Erdos
Joseph Erdos III
Joseph Erdos II
Lerae Ettienne
Nicole Evans
Chris Evans
Zach Fabel
Phil Faccone
Rudy Favard
Chris Fee
Rory Feeney
Kelyn Fillmore
Alec Finelli
Alec Finney
Keaton Flint
Carmen Flores
James Flores
Lydia Flores
Jordan Flores
Malcolm Floyd
Tyler Foehr
James Foley
Jim Foley
Cheryl Folks
Leslie Folks
Leslie Cole Folks
Stephen Forchion
Robin Elaine Forchion
Traci Forchion
Russell Forchion

Russell Forchion Jr.

Jason Forcier

Connor Frizzell

Phil Gaetano

Alexis Galetka

Ethan Gambale

Chris Gambella

Emily Gardner

Matt Gardner

Dan Gary

Joe Gatto

Alexis Geletka

Caleb Gelsomino

Nick Gentile

Elias Gharios

Anthony Giagunto

Dennis Gibson

Ka'Lial Glaud

Anthony Glaud

Zachari Glover

Steven Glowiak

Tim Godfrey

Kevin Goldsmith

Brendan Goldup

Tim Goodwin

Chris Goodwin

Ronnie Gordon

Paul Gorham

Chris Gough

Zach Grant

Curtis Grant

Nicholas Grasso

Paul Graziadei

Marcus Gregory

Emily Grobmyer

Paul Guarino

Ryan Gunningsmith

Rose Hadsell

Micky Haller

Delonce Hargrave

Eddie Harper (Father)

Eddie Harper (Son)

Marquis Harper

Christine Harper

Brandon Harris

Marcus Harris

Wayne Harris

Alvetrice Harris

LaQuay Hawkins

Bob Healey

Tyriq Heart-Mills

Brock Hecking

David Heim

Noe Hernandez

Harold Hill

Ann Hill

Karen Hill

Greg Hill

Raqia Hill

Rosa Hill

Mehki Hill

Eric Hill

Wesley Hill

Tiffany Hill

Tarius Hill

Khaliyafa Hill

Cleo Hill

D. A. Hinton

Ray Hodgson

Matt Hoffman

Albert Holmes

Pearl Holmes

Leslie Holmes

Joan Holmes

Harold Holmes

Matt Holzer

Garrett Hood

Sandra Hooks

A'laam Horne

Salaam Horne

Jade Howard

Charlie Huff

June Humes

Rob Humes

Olivia Hurd

Brad Hurlbut

Sisilyn Hutchinson

Brandon Hutchinson

Chris Hutton

Gregory Ibe

Matt Ilalio

Fenumiai Ilalio

Therese Ilalio

Osedebamen Imeokparia

Bill Inge

Desha L. Jackson

Kelsey Jacoby

PJ James

Jo Jo Jamiel

Ryan Janoska

Jim Jeffers

Evan Jobst

Bobby Johnson

Robert Johnson

Bret Johnson

Tim Johnson

Brandon Johnson

Ryan Jonaska

Brandon Jones

Denzel Jones

Greg Jones

Meah Jones

Michael Joyce II

Ruthann Joyce

Michael Joyce

Thomas Joyce

Elias Karam

Leo Katsetos

Jeff Keffer

Evan Kelley

Theo Kelly

John Kelly

Justin Kennedy

Dusty Kessler

Sean Kessler

Jackson King

Jason King

Jane Kitchen

Tom Kitchen

Alex Kitchen

Madison Kohl

Vince Kowalski

Hunter Krajewski	Danny Macaluso
Doug Kramer	Gregory Madrid
Chris Kulesza	Craig Mager
Erin L. Murphy	Tom Mahoney
Ryan Ladson	Silvio Maione
Kyle Lafferty	Zach Major
Josh Lambo	Tony Malone
Brady Larson	Chris Mandas
Darnell Laws	Justin Mandela
Trymaine Lee	Mike Maniscalco
Nick Leiningen	John Maniscalco
Humberto Leigue	Adam Marcucci
Shane Lennon	Kaitlyn Marrie
Bill Leopold	Justin Martel
Keemie Lewis	Frank Martin
Kaiwan Lewis	Julian Martin
Anthony Libby	Tammy Martin
Kathleen Lieblich	Jaime Martinez
Paul Link	Karen Mason
Matt Linnehan	Charlie Massey
Tim Little	Christopher Mastrocola
James Litton	Rick Mauriello
Corey Litton	Michael Mazzeo
Darlene Litton	Jenn Mazzo
Mike Livingston	Sam McCain
Brandon Locher	Ryan McCarthy
Chris Lombardi	Frank McConnell
Johanna Lopez	Lian McDonough
Roy Lucas	Kieran McGirl
Domenick Luongo	Jake McGlinchey
Brandon Lynard	Matt McGlynn
Justin Lynch	Mike McGough
Daniel Lynch	Joseph McGuckin

Kordel McInnis

Rueben McIntosh

Allen McMurren

Kimberlyn Mele

E. J. Melton

Victoria Mendoza

Sean Merrill

Alex Michael

Desmond Mighty

Jeremy Miles

Tyler Miller

Kyle Miller

Anthony Milone

Mario Miranda

Allison Mockler

Michael Montemurro

Eric Mooney

Ricky Moore Jr.

Josh Moore

Greg Moore

Troy Moore

Bill Mortelitte

Kathy Mortelitte

Gary Mortelitte

Christian Mortelitte

Peyton Mortellite

Ryan Mueller

Lawrence Nemhard

RJ Noel

Mark Nofri

Matt Norman

Mary Norwood

Yolanda Norwood

Galen Norwood Sr.

Galen Norwood Jr.

Rashaad and Matt (Only NY)

Steve O'Brien

Andrew O'Neill

Coley O'Brien

Nick O'Brien

Jason O'Brien

Kimmie O'Brien

Chris O'Connor

Joe O'Neill

Pat O'Neill

Sean O'Neill

Andrew O'Neill

Kevin O'Sullivan

Jim Olayos

Shea Olayos

Paul Ordille

Joanne Ordille

Andrew Ordille

Luke Ordille

Rocco Ordille

Giuseppe Ottaiano

Yolanda Oviede-Hill

Paul Pabst

Michael Page

David A. Palmieri

Kyle Pantalone

Marcus Papas

Charles Pardini

Brett Parenteau

Matt Parmenter

John Parmenter III

Cejai Parrish
Chaz Partosan
CJ Parvelus
Kerri Patton
Phil Paulhill Jr.
Phil Paulhill Sr.
Arlene Paulhill
Greg Pease
Miles Pease
Jeffrey Peras Jr.
Andrew Perloff
Valentino Perrina
David Perry
Sean Peters
Julian Peterson
Jayden Peterson
Jyi Peterson
Tesha Peterson
Ernest Pettway
Adrian Phillips
Evan Pittman
Jasmine Pittman
Jason Plescow
Eli Pogue
Dan Polaski
Brett Polinsky
Will Polite
Kemoy Powell
Graling Primas
Progressly
Casey Pullybank
Joel Quintong
Nathan Racicot

Chris Rader
George Ragos
Chris Ragos
Matt Ramos
Ricardo Ramsay
Monica Re
Palmer Reap III
Palmer Reap IV
Vincenzo Recine
Dr. Michael Redler
Vincent Reed
Austin Regalbuto
Dennis Regan
Gary Reho
Alex Relph
James Rentz
Cassidy Reynolds
Kaheem Reynolds
Norma Richardson
Andrew Roach
Brandon Robertson
Durell Robinson
Chris Rodgers
Steve Rodio
Chris Rogers
Bill Romaniello
Jamie Romeo
Kelsey Rondeau
Lowell Rose
Jamie Ross
Rich Rossi
Jim Roth
Matthew Rousseau

Jean-Daniel Roussel
Tim Rumpff
Jennifer Russell
Dan Russoman
Mike Rutigliano
Makenna Sacco
Mike Sacco
Paul Sacco Jr.
Charles Sacco
Carlina Sacco
Judy Sacco
Peggy Sacco
Jon Sam
Mike Samela
Cody Sampson
Sam Sanford
Thomas Sanford
Sarah Sanford
Preston Sanford
Donya Sanford
Paul Sanford
Pat Saporito
Joe Sarnese
Shane Scambray
Stephen Scarpati
Zachary Schafer
Ryan Scherer
Duane Schilling
Brad Schilling
Adam Schroeder
Matt Schuler
Justin Sexton
Christian Shanafelt

John Shannon
Bruce Shaw
Jack Sheehan
Joe Shelton
Katie Shepard
Robert Shepherd
Brad Shilling
Zach Short
Josh Shuart
Niko Sierra
Alyssa Silipino
Matt Silvesti
Ryan Simone
Brendon Slade
Smiley
Bryce Smith
Darryl Smith
Mac Smith
Mark Smith
John Snee IV
Christian Snowden
Christian Sobin
Mike Somogy
Victor Sorrento
Harold Spears
Keshaudas Spence
Kim Spence
Kellen Sperduto
Mike Stalba
Paul Stanton
Danielle Steen
Robert Steffe
Sandra Stevenson

Kevin Stimmel
Matt Sullivan
Jayson Sullivan
Zac Sullivan
Matt Szczur
Julian Talley
Ivan Tamba
Dom Tartaglia
Rock Tate
Mike Tavani
David Taylor
Drew Terry
Eddie Testa
Alex Testani
Todd Thomas
Stephan Thomas
Robert Thompson
Brad Tiernan
John Todoro
Ronnie Tolbert
Mark Tomaszewski
Q. Townsel
Matt Trainor
Kevin Troilo
Max Trudeau
Tavares Tuck
Dr. Brad Tucker
Joe Tulino
Zak Turner
Ross Uglem
Harry Ulmer
Live from the Middle Urinal
Mike Vaccarella

Jon Valentine
Max Valles
Paul Valles
Andre Valles
Hakeem Valles
Pamela Valles
Nick Valori
Mario Valori
RaKendrick Varnado
Ralph S. Ventre
Perry Vitali
Brian Vitols
Beth Anne Voight-Jause
Robert Volk
Garrett Wadsworth
John Wagner
Kelvin Wagner
Hunter Warner
Chiyonte Warren
Gabby Washington
Carl Watson
Devante Waugh
Moses Webb
Jordan Weiss
Caroline Wells
Jon Wexler
Mike Whalen
Norman White
Michael Whitney
Lamont Whitstyne
Adam Widmeier
James Wildason
Tyler Wilhelm

Damon Williford
Brittany Williams
Ron Williams
Woody Williams
Rasheed Williams
Derek Williams
Rob Williamson
Ryan Wills
Bobby Wilson
Stacey Wilson
TaMaric Wilson
Luke Wischnowski
Dave Wissman
Kyle Wolf
Madison Worthington
Gary Martin Worthington Jr.
Donovan Worthington
Gerald Mark Worthington
Gary Worthington Sr.
Toni Worthington
Dante Worthington
Kayla Worthington
Rachel Worthington
Raeven Worthington
Gordon Michael Worthington
Blair Worthington
Giana Worthington
Dimitri Worthington
Jill Worthington
Londyn Worthington
Esperanza Worthington
Alberto Worthington
Kiana Worthington

Dominique Worthington
Esperanza I. Worthington
Bronx Worthington
Morgan Worthington
Thomas Worthington
Javier Worthington
Steven Worthington
Sobrina Worthington
Skylar Wylie
Dejour Young
Michael Zambarano
Cameron Ziny

Special Thanks:
Mom
Jarret Bragg
Courtland Bragg
Nicole Evans
Kia Marie Dawkins
Emily Gardner
Kelyn Fillmore
Sean Dougherty

Made in the USA
Columbia, SC
03 August 2018